Walter de la Mare SELECTED POEMS

This item must be returned or renewed on or before the latest date shown

WITHDRAWN FROM STOCK

SEFTON PUBLIC LIBRARIES

FAX: 0151 934 5770

A fine will be charged on any overdue item plus the cost of reminders sent

*by the same author*

COMPLETE POEMS
PEACOCK PIE: A BOOK OF RHYMES
SHORT STORIES 1895–1926
SHORT STORIES 1927–1956
SHORT STORIES FOR CHILDREN

# Walter de la Mare SELECTED POEMS

*Edited by* MATTHEW SWEENEY

*faber and faber*

First published in 2006
by Faber and Faber Limited
3 Queen Square London WC1N 3AU

Photoset by RefineCatch Ltd, Bungay, Suffolk
Printed in England by T.J. International Ltd, Padstow, Cornwall

A CIP record for this book
is available from the British Library

ISBN 978-0-571-21044-2
    0-571-21044-9

10 9 8 7 6 5 4 3 2 1

# Contents

Introduction  xi

Tartary  3
John Mouldy  4
The Fly  4
The Silver Penny  5
Reverie  6
The Three Beggars  7
The Miller and His Son  8
The Ogre  10
The Fiddlers  12
Haunted  13
Captain Lean  14
The Raven's Tomb  15
The Funeral  15
Come!  16
The Winter-Boy  17
They Told Me  18
The Children of Stare  19
The Birthnight: To F  20
Napoleon  20
Echo  21
Autumn  21
The Scarecrow  22
Nod  23
Winter  24
All That's Past  25
Never More Sailor  25
Arabia  26
Never-to-Be  27

The Listeners  28
Winter Dusk  29
An Epitaph  30
Alas, Alack!  31
The Huntsmen  31
Some One  32
Old Shellover  32
Jim Jay  33
Miss T.  34
Mistletoe  34
The Lost Shoe  35
The Sea Boy  36
Off the Ground  37
Late  41
King David  42
Nicholas Nye  42
The Pigs and the Charcoal-Burner  44
Five Eyes  44
The Old Stone House  45
The Changeling  45
Bewitched  47
Silver  48
The Song of Soldiers  48
A Song of Enchantment  49
Dream-Song  50
The Song of the Mad Prince  50
Alone  51
Mistress Fell  52
The Ghost  53
The Stranger  54
The Marionettes  55
The Three Strangers  56
The Scribe  56

Fare Well 57
The Comb 58
The Moth 59
Titmouse 59
The Veil 60
The Suicide 61
Good-Bye 61
The Corner Stone 62
The Familiar 63
Sunk Lyonesse 64
Who? 64
Bitter Waters 65
Crazed 66
Nat Vole 66
John Virgin 67
Chrystopher Orcherdson 67
Richard Halladay 67
Thomas Logge 68
O Passer-By, Beware! 688
The Shubble 68
Bones 69
Hi! 69
Seeds 70
As I Went to the Well-Head 70
Peeping Tom 71
The Feckless Dinner-Party 73
Comfort 75
Good Company 76
The Railway Junction 79
Full Circle 80
Tom's Angel 80
A Robin 82
The Snowdrop 82

Quack  84
Oh, Yes, my Dear  84
Seen and Heard  85
'Please to Remember'  85
Dry August Burned  86
At Ease  87
Clavicord  87
Faint Music  88
Martins: September  88
Swallows Flown  89
The Old Summerhouse  89
Rooks in October  90
The Last Arrow  90
Snow  92
Crops  93
Done For  93
The Old Sailor  94
Pooh!  95
Ever  96
Lob-Lie-by-the-Fire  97
The Snowflake  97
The Bead Mat  98
The Border Bird  99
The Song of Seven  100
Will-o'-the-Wisp  101
Nothing  102
Then as Now  102
Under the Rose  103
Israfel  104
The Burning-Glass  104
Swifts  105
The Field  106
The Blind Boy  106

The Owl  107
Once  108
The Dead Jay  109
Eureka  110
Birds in Winter  112
Empty  112
'Said Flores'  113
Joy  114
Solitude  115
Martins  116
The Plaster Cast  117
The Last Swallow  117
The Spotted Flycatcher  117
Blondin  118
Slim Cunning Hands  118
'It Was the Last Time He Was Seen Alive'  119
Winter Evening  119
An Old Cannon  120
In a Churchyard  120
Tarbury Steep  121
Ulladare  121
De Profundis  122
The Minstrel  122
Tat for Tit  123
The China Cat  123
Le Jeu est Fait  124

# Introduction

In a preface to a 1982 edition of Walter de la Mare's novel *Memoirs of a Midget*, his best-known prose work, Angela Carter said that its author's reputation 'as a poet and writer for adults has softly and silently vanished away since his death in 1956'. Any lover of the poetry or prose encountering this would have found it a stark pronouncement, but would have been appeased somewhat by the new edition of the novel. Things have not improved much over the twenty-odd years since, though the publication of the adult stories in two volumes, in 1996 and 2001, was to be welcomed, reminding us how enduringly good those stories can be (and how excellent it would be to have a selection of the best of them). It is sincerely to be hoped that this selection will do the same and more for the poetry – the poetry aimed at adults, I should say, because as the above Carter quote implies, the children's poetry is another matter, *Peacock Pie* being perennially in print and popular. I suspect, though, that the only adult poem of de la Mare's that most readers of poetry today will know is the well-anthologised 'The Listeners'.

The idea of being known by a single poem is a thing of horror to most poets, second only to being completely forgotten. Yeats, for example, came to loathe 'The Lake Isle of Innisfree', and any anthologist will tell you that there are contemporary poets who prefer to be excluded than to be represented by the one poem of theirs everybody knows. All poets like to feel they're evolving, and can't be summed up by one particular type of poem, and particularly not by one title. The fact that not all poets do continue to improve, and that for some there are clear peaks (Coleridge being a particularly good example to mention here, simply because he was so dear to de la Mare) rising from the lower territory that comprises the greater body of their work, is of no consolation to most of us. I am not aware if Walter de la Mare ever came to dislike 'The Listeners' because of its popularity but I hope not, as the poem is central to his work in a way that Yeats' poem is not. It is also a poem that has been admired by many poets – Frost, for example, who was very taken with the poem's versification.

I first knew only 'The Listeners' from de la Mare's work – it was that poem, in fact (as well as two of Yeats' early fairy poems), that got me interested in poetry initially, at the age of ten or eleven. I loved the mystery of it, the ghosts that populate it, the vividness of the dramatic scene:

But only a host of phantom listeners
   That dwelt in the lone house then
Stood listening in the quiet of the moonlight
   To that voice from the world of men:
Stood thronging the faint moonbeams on the dark stair,
   That goes down to the empty hall,
Hearkening in an air stirred and shaken
   By the lonely Traveller's call.

And a trawl through the *Complete Poems* will reveal how many of the poems evoke this mysterious, ghostly, world of the dead. (The same is true of his wonderful stories, much admired by Graham Greene, and again way out of fashion.) Within its pages I encountered fairies, ghosts, changelings, witches, wraiths, wizards, shades, angels, nereids and seraphs. And one is as likely to come across these beings in the children's poems as in the adult. Here is the opening of one of the children's poems, 'John Mouldy':

I spied John Mouldy in his cellar,
Deep down twenty steps of stone;
In the dusk he sat a-smiling,
    Smiling there alone.

He read no book, he snuffed no candle;
The rats ran in, the rats ran out;
And far and near, the drips of water
    Went whisp'ring about.

It is the world of folk-tales and fairytales (like poor old Jim
Jay who got 'stuck fast in yesterday'), and the anonymous
ballads – an alternative world, more alive, paradoxically,
than the world of living humans. A dream world, one might
say – and Dream even appears personified in one of the
poems. Dreams were always important for de la Mare. 'Why
should we prefer the waking experience?', he is recorded as
asking in one of a series of conversations in old age with the
neurologist Russell Brain (collected in *Tea with Walter de la
Mare*). 'Isn't a dream just as real?' Another, not unrelated
question jotted down by Brain was 'What is the difference
between being childish and childlike? Is not the persistence
of some qualities of childhood into adult life, and even old
age, often a sign of genius? I think we should have a new
word for childhood.' Childhood, for de la Mare, was the
peak of human existence, and a favourite thesis of his,
which he repeated frequently, was that children come into
the world fully equipped with much that they do not learn,
and possess an intuition, as well as a natural grace of
movement, which they subsequently lose.

A childlike vision is present throughout de la Mare's work,
not just in the writing for children, and his biographer,
Theresa Whistler, records how he continued deliberately to
exercise the special faculties of childhood – daydreaming,

make-believe, questioning that takes nothing for granted. 'Make believe', he declared, was always to him 'one of the richest of human consolations'.

Walter de la Mare's childhood was spent in suburban London. Born in 1873, in Charlton, Kent, his father, James Edward Delamare (the original spelling of the name which Walter – or Jack, as he was known within the family – would subsequently change) was an official of the Bank of England. The main bond he formed as a child was with his mother Lucy Sophia, who introduced him to the world of traditional fairytales and storytelling. This was invaluable to an imaginative child such as him, and proved central to his gift throughout his life.

His first poetry collection, the children's volume *Songs of Childhood*, appeared under the pseudonym Walter Ramal, in 1902, but when a group of poems was taken by the *Monthly Review*, its editor, Henry Newbolt, persuaded him to publish under his real name. The love of anonymity never left him, however. As late as 1918 he copied down an epitaph from Zennor churchyard, noting that the author was the famous Mr Anon, and wishing that he were Mr Anon, 'unknown, beloved, perennial, ubiquitous, in that wide shady hat of his and dark dwelling eyes'.

In 1908 Newbolt helped de la Mare get a grant of £200 from the Prime Minister, and this allowed him to resign from the Anglo-American Oil Company, in which he had worked for eighteen years. From now on he could throw himself into his writing, and he began producing poems that would be included later in *The Listeners* and *Peacock Pie*, adult and children's collections, respectively, that appeared only a year apart, in 1912 and 1913.

Just before this, in 1911, a new anthology was published with the intention of reviving the public interest in poetry.

The editor was Sir Edward Marsh, and he suggested the label 'Georgian' for this new poetry. It was a startling public success, so much so that a second Georgian anthology quickly followed, and five volumes in all were published between 1911 and 1922. De la Mare was prominently featured and although this helped enormously to widen his public, he was not so closely identified with the Georgian school as to sink with it when it went into disfavour. Enough readers could see that he was not typical, and had strengths that transcended most of the other poets grouped under the banner. Pound, who disliked equally all the Georgians, made 'solitary and surprising' exceptions of de la Mare and W. H. Davies. And for Nabokov, de la Mare and Rupert Brooke stood out from the rest. Of the other Georgian poets, it was Brooke de la Mare valued most – as much for his personality as for his poetry. In a memorial tribute after Brooke's untimely death in 1915, de la Mare mentioned that in one of his travel papers Brooke had described the city of Quebec as having 'the radiance and-repose of an immortal' – 'That in so many words', wrote de la Mare, 'brings back his living remembrance. With him there was a happy shining impression that he must have just come – that very moment – from another planet, one well within the solar system but a little more like Utopia than ours.'

Together, *The Listeners* and *Peacock Pie* brought de la Mare more attention and success than any subsequent publication was to bring. The plaudits he got would be the envy of any writer. Edmund Gosse, on being sent *The Listeners*, wrote that he was 'charmed with the music and the fancy, and with the delicate, high, pure region of feeling in which your poetry moves'. Edward Thomas, who had been slow to warm to the early work but would become his biggest and – for Newbolt – most important supporter, wrote about the same book, 'You might as well ask me to write a poem myself as to write about these. Each one takes me a little deeper into a world I seem to know just for the moment as well as you – only not really knowing it I cannot write.'

Here is one of those poems, 'An Epitaph', in full:

Here lies a most beautiful lady,
Light of step and heart was she;
I think she was the most beautiful lady
That ever was in the West Country

But beauty vanishes; beauty passes;
However rare – rare it be;
And when I crumble, who will remember
This lady of the West Country?

And this is Yeats' comment on it: 'There is not an original sentence in this poem, yet it will live for centuries.'

As with all his books, however, he'd been reluctant to give the poems up for publication, since after this point he could do no more tinkering with them. For a poet who valued the unconscious mind over the conscious, he was an inveterate reviser. When told that Constable had taken *The Listeners* and *Peacock Pie* he wrote in a letter: 'I think I must feel something like the little boy who sees the poor rabbit he has petted and fed brought in smoking on a dish. I didn't want them killed and I wanted them much nicer!'

It is difficult, given the neglect into which his work has fallen, to realise just how much de la Mare was valued by his peers. For Frost, 'He was one of those I thought really *was* one [a poet]. I pretend that about some of them socially.' Hardy (who was one of the few writers who really affected him – Poe and James were the others) in a letter praised his poems, '. . . those delightful sensations of moonlight and forests and haunted houses which I myself seem to have visited, curiously enough.' The hard-to-please American poet and critic, Randall Jarrell, has this to say of his imaginative territory: 'De la Mare's world is neither the best nor the worst but the most enchanted of all possible worlds. It assures us that if reality is not necessarily what we should like it to be, it is necessarily what we feel it to be . . .; if de la Mare happened to develop a taste for science, a whole new category of reality would suddenly come into being . . . The man who would wish him a different writer would wish the Great Snowy Owl at the zoo a goose, so as to eat it for Christmas.' This would have pleased de la Mare, who asserted once that the free play of the imagination might be 'the outcome of a thirst for a reality distinct from the actual', and on another occasion confessed in a letter that 'Now and again over one's mind comes the glamour of a kind of visionary world saturating this'.

At the same time, there is another side to de la Mare's work, full of what appears to be a more conventional reality, and dealing with the world we know. I'm talking of his many poems that touch on birds, animals and natural phenomena. But even these have about them, as Theresa Whistler points out, 'a peculiar visionary intensity and a marked lack of the true countryman's or naturalist's informed detail'. She goes on to echo what some of de la Mare's earlier admirers had felt, that his detail 'had something in common with Pre-Raphaelite detail: a jewelled hallucinatory intensity'.

Here is the third stanza of 'Winter', from *The Listeners*:

Thick draws the dark,
    And spark by spark,
The frost-fires kindle, and soon
Over that sea of frozen foam
    Floats the white moon.

One of de la Mare's most obviously striking qualities, as
these lines make clear, is his perfect ear and staggering
technical assurance – and that slight unpredictability of
rhythm Frost was so curious about in 'The Listeners'. In his
introduction to a 1963 selection, Auden put it like this:
'One might say that, in every poet, there dwells an Ariel,
who sings, and a Prospero, who comprehends, but in any
particular poem, sometimes even in the whole work of a
particular poet, one of the partners plays a greater role than
the other. Though the role of Prospero in de la Mare's poetry
is much greater than one may realise on a first reading it
would not be unfair, I think, to call him an Ariel-dominated
poet. Certainly, his most obvious virtues, those which no
reader can fail to see immediately, are verbal and formal, the
delicacy of his metrical fingering and the graceful
architecture of his stanzas . . . The reader's ear is continually
excited by rhythmical variations without ever losing a sense
of the underlying pattern.'

Another comment of Auden's, on a separate occasion –
when he was responding to the wonderful anthology 'for the
young of all ages' that de la Mare edited, *Come Hither* –
may be worth making here: 'Poetry does not need to be great
or even serious to be good.' Auden made no distinction in
value between children's poetry and adult, de la Mare's own
or otherwise. In the above-mentioned introduction to the
1963 selection he wrote, 'it must never be forgotten that,
while there are some good poems which are only for adults,
because they pre-suppose adult experience in their readers,
there are no good poems which are only for children.'
I agree, but as anyone who writes for both children and
adults will find out, de la Mare's children's poetry affected
his adult poetry. To a contemporary eye, the earlier
*Songs of Childhood* is still fresh, whereas the bulk of

*Poems* (1906) seems now didactic and dated, and straining after a seriousness that the author obviously felt a book intended for adults had to have. What children demand, however – inventiveness and music, and a lightness of touch – was much more in keeping with de la Mare's gifts, and the next adult collection, *The Listeners*, incorporated a lot of those qualities, and as a consequence the gap between it and *Peacock Pie* is not nearly so great.

Another thing that separates de la Mare from most poets is that all through his writing career he also wrote prose seriously, and this too affected his poetry. Look, for a start, at how many of the poems are stories as well, and although the ballads and fairytales he'd always loved may have a lot to do with this, there must also, inevitably, be a cross-influence from the stories he wrote in prose. It is noticeable, too, that he took on board more from the prose writers of the 1890s than from the poets. And he himself made a more startling connection between poetry and prose, in general, when he said, 'It is in prose rather than in fine verse that the poet is likely to discover both novel and subtle rhythms which a little or much delicate contriving will convert into the most promising and seductive of metres.'

Is it possible, then, to identify the reason why de la Mare's star has so fallen? There were some dissenting voices at the time of his greatest success. Edith Sitwell, despite once telling him that he and Yeats had been the two inspirations of her youth, on another occasion dismissed his work as charming but slight. Eliot, at a memorial reading held by the Arts Council soon after his death, said he always thought of de la Mare's poetry as chamber music – but the best kind of chamber music. Perhaps, during the period of modernism and afterwards, his poetry was deemed too quiet, too small – too outdated. De la Mare was never in the slightest bit interested in poetry fashions. He ignored stylistic changes around him and kept using inversions and 'thou' and 'thee' when nobody else was doing so any more. He made only minor concessions to the colloquial in his poetry – unlike his prose. His books, from *The Listeners* and *Peacock Pie* on (this goes for the collections of stories, as well) were very uneven, which never helps a reputation, but in each there were poems as good as any he had written. Over half of my selection comes from *Motley* (1918), *The Veil* (1921), *Ding Dong Bell* (1924), *The Fleeting* (1933), *Memory* (1938), *Bells and Grass* (1941, for children), *The Burning-Glass* (1945), *Inward Companion* (1950) and *O Lovely England* (1953). I have left alone the two long poems written late in his life, *The Traveller* (1946) and *Winged Chariot* (1951), as I could not see anything I could usefully extract. As far as the writing of my introduction is concerned, particularly the biographical details, I am indebted to Theresa Whistler's excellent biography, *Imagination of the Heart: The Life of Walter de la Mare* (Duckworth, 1993).

It is to be hoped that picking the best of the poems out and grouping them together in this selection will remind some readers – and show many more for the first time – just how fine and varied this work is, and how all of it emanates from an imaginative world that is timeless and completely distinctive. I have taken my cue from Auden and mixed up the adult and the children's work. The selection is arranged chronologically, and has been made through a contemporary reader's eye, in the hope of showing the work in a fresh light.

Information about the Walter de la Mare Society is available on the website www.bluetree.co.uk/wdlmsociety.

Matthew Sweeney

Walter de la Mare SELECTED POEMS

# Tartary

If I were Lord of Tartary,
　Myself, and me alone,
My bed should be of ivory,
　Of beaten gold my throne;
And in my court should peacocks flaunt,
And in my forests tigers haunt,
And in my pools great fishes slant
　　Their fins athwart the sun.

If I were Lord of Tartary,
　Trumpeters every day
To all my meals should summon me,
　And in my courtyards bray;
And in the evening lamps should shine,
Yellow as honey, red as wine,
While harp, and flute, and mandoline
　　Made music sweet and gay.

If I were Lord of Tartary,
　I'd wear a robe of beads,
White, and gold, and green they'd be –
　And small and thick as seeds;
And ere should wane the morning star,
I'd don my robe and scimitar,
And zebras seven should draw my car
　　Through Tartary's dark glades.

Lord of the fruits of Tartary,
　Her rivers silver-pale!
Lord of the hills of Tartary,
　Glen, thicket, wood, and dale!

Her flashing stars, her scented breeze,
Her trembling lakes, like foamless seas,
Her bird-delighting citron-trees,
    In every purple vale!


## John Mouldy

I spied John Mouldy in his cellar,
Deep down twenty steps of stone;
In the dusk he sat a-smiling,
    Smiling there alone.

He read no book, he snuffed no candle;
The rats ran in, the rats ran out;
And far and near, the drip of water
    Went whisp'ring about.

The dusk was still, with dew a-falling,
I saw the Dog-star bleak and grim,
I saw a slim brown rat of Norway
    Creep over him.

I spied John Mouldy in his cellar,
Deep down twenty steps of stone;
In the dusk he sat a-smiling,
    Smiling there alone.


## The Fly

How large unto the tiny fly
    Must little things appear! –
A rosebud like a feather bed,
    Its prickle like a spear;

A dewdrop like a looking-glass,
    A hair like golden wire;
The smallest grain of mustard-seed
    As fierce as coals of fire;

A loaf of bread, a lofty hill;
    A wasp, a cruel leopard;
And specks of salt as bright to see
    As lambkins to a shepherd.


## The Silver Penny

'Sailorman, I'll give to you
    My bright silver penny,
If out to sea you'll sail me
    And my dear sister Jenny.'

'Get in, young sir, I'll sail ye
    And your dear sister Jenny,
But pay she shall her golden locks
    Instead of your penny.'

They sail away, they sail away,
    O fierce the winds blew!
The foam flew in clouds
    And dark the night grew!

And all the green sea-water
    Climbed steep into the boat;
Back to the shore again
    Sail they will not.

Drowned is the sailorman,
    Drowned is sweet Jenny,

And drowned in the deep sea
   A bright silver penny.


## Reverie

When slim Sophia mounts her horse
   And paces down the avenue,
It seems an inward melody
     She paces to.

Each narrow hoof is lifted high
   Beneath the dark enclustering pines,
A silver ray within his bit
     And bridle shines.

His eye burns deep, his tail is arched,
   And streams upon the shadowy air,
The daylight sleeks his jetty flanks,
     His mistress' hair.

Her habit flows in darkness down,
   Upon the stirrup rests her foot,
Her brow is lifted, as if earth
     She heeded not.

'Tis silent in the avenue,
   The sombre pines are mute of song,
The blue is dark, there moves no breeze
     The boughs among.

When slim Sophia mounts her horse
   And paces down the avenue,
It seems an inward melody
     She paces to.

# The Three Beggars

'Twas autumn daybreak gold and wild
   While past St. Ann's grey tower they shuffled
Three beggars spied a fairy-child
   In crimson mantle muffled.

The daybreak lighted up her face
   All pink, and sharp, and emerald-eyed;
She looked on them a little space,
   And shrill as hautboy cried: –

'O three tall footsore men in rags
   Which walking this gold morn I see,
What will ye give me from your bags
   For fairy kisses three?'

The first, that was a reddish man,
   Out of his bundle takes a crust:
'La, by the tombstones of St. Ann
   There's fee, if fee ye must!'

The second, that was a chestnut man,
   Out of his bundle draws a bone:
'La, by the belfry of St. Ann,
   And all my breakfast gone!'

The third, that was a yellow man,
   Out of his bundle picks a groat,
'La, by the Angel of St. Ann,
   And I must go without.'

That changeling, lean and icy-lipped,
   Touched crust, and bone, and groat, and lo!
Beneath her finger taper-tipped
   The magic all ran through.

Instead of crust a peacock pie,
    Instead of bone sweet venison,
Instead of groat a white lily
        With seven blooms thereon.

And each fair cup was deep with wine:
    Such was the changeling's charity
The sweet feast was enough for nine,
        But not too much for three.

O toothsome meat in jelly froze!
    O tender haunch of elfin stag!
Oh, rich the odour that arose!
        Oh, plump with scraps each bag!

There, in the daybreak gold and wild,
    Each merry-hearted beggar man
Drank deep unto the fairy child,
        And blessed the good St. Ann.


## The Miller and His Son

A twangling harp for Mary,
    A silvery flute for John,
And now we'll play the livelong day,
    'The Miller and his Son.' . . .

'The Miller went a-walking
    All in the forest high,
He sees three doves a-flitting
    Against the dark blue sky:

'Says he, "My son, now follow
    These doves so white and free,

That cry above the forest,
    And surely cry to thee."

' "I go, my dearest Father,
    But Oh! I sadly fear,
These doves so white will lead me far,
    But never bring me near."

'He kisses the Miller,
    He cries, "Awhoop to ye!"
And straightway through the forest
    Follows the wood-doves three.

'There came a sound of weeping
    To the Miller in his Mill;
Red roses in a thicket
    Bloomed over near his wheel;

'Three stars shone wild and brightly
    Above the forest dim:
But never his dearest son
    Returns again to him.

'The cuckoo shall call "Cuckoo!"
    In vain along the vale,
The linnet, and the blackbird,
    The mournful nightingale;

'The Miller hears and sees not,
    He's thinking of his son;
His toppling wheel is silent;
    His grinding done.

' "O doves so white!" he weepeth,
    "O roses on the tree!
O stars that shine so brightly –
    You shine in vain for me!

' "I bade him, 'Follow, follow';
   He said, 'O Father dear,
These doves so white will lead me far
   But never bring me near!' " ' . . .

A twangling harp for Mary,
   A silvery flute for John,
And now we'll play the livelong day,
   'The Miller and his Son.'


## The Ogre

'Tis moonlight on Trebarwith Sands,
   And moonlight on their seas,
Lone in a cove a cottage stands
   Enclustered in with trees.

Snuffing its thin faint smoke afar
   An Ogre prowls, and he
Smells supper; for where humans are,
   Rich dainties too may be.

Sweet as a larder to a mouse,
   So to him staring down,
Seemed the small-windowed moonlit house,
   With jasmine overgrown.

He snorted, as the billows snort
   In darkness of the night,
Betwixt his lean locks tawny-swart
   He glowered on the sight.

Into the garden sweet with peas
   He put his wooden shoe,

And bending back the apple trees
    Crept covetously through;

Then, stooping, with an impious eye
    Stared through the lattice small,
And spied two children which did lie
    Asleep, against the wall.

Into their dreams no shadow fell
    Of his disastrous thumb
Groping discreet, and gradual,
    Across the quiet room.

But scarce his nail had scraped the cot
    Wherein these children lay,
As if his malice were forgot,
    It suddenly did stay.

For faintly in the ingle-nook
    He heard a cradle-song,
That rose into his thoughts and woke
    Terror them among.

For she who in the kitchen sat
    Darning by the fire,
Guileless of what he would be at,
    Sang sweet as wind or wire: –

'Lullay, thou little tiny child
    By-by, lullay, lullie;
Jesu in glory, meek and mild,
    This night remember thee!

'Fiend, witch, and goblin, foul and wild,
    He deems them smoke to be;
Lullay, thou little tiny child,
    By-by, lullay, lullie!'

The Ogre lifted up his eyes
    Into the moon's pale ray,
And gazed upon her leopard-wise,
    Cruel and clear as day;

He snarled in gluttony and fear –
    The wind blows dismally –
'Jesu in storm my lambs be near,
    By-by, lullay, lullie!'

And like a ravenous beast which sees
    The hunter's icy eye,
So did this wretch in wrath confess
    Sweet Jesu's mastery.

With gaunt locks dangling, crouched he, then
    Drew backward from his prey,
Through tangled apple-boughs again
    He wrenched and rent his way.

Out on Trebarwith Sands he broke,
    The waves yelled back his cry,
Gannet and cormorant echo woke
    As he went striding by.


## The Fiddlers

Nine feat Fiddlers had good Queen Bess
To play her music as she did dress.
Behind an arras of horse and hound
They sate there scraping delightsome sound.
Spangled, bejewelled, her skirts would she
Draw o'er a petticoat of cramasie;
And soft each string like a bird would sing

In the starry dusk of evening.
Then slow from the deeps the crisscross bows,
Crooning like doves, arose and arose.
When, like a cage, did her ladies raise
A stiff rich splendour o'er her ribbed stays,
Like bumbling bees those four times nine
Fingers in melodies loud did pine;
Last came her coif and her violet shoon
And her virgin face shone out like the moon:
Oh, then in a rapture those three times three
Fiddlers squealed shrill on their topmost C.


## Haunted

From out the wood I watched them shine, —
    The windows of the haunted house,
Now ruddy as enchanted wine,
    Now dark as flittermouse.

There went a thin voice piping airs
    Along the grey and crooked walks, —
A garden of thistledown and tares,
    Bright leaves, and giant stalks.

The twilight rain shone at its gates,
    Where long-leaved grass in shadow grew;
And back in silence to her mates
    A voiceless raven flew.

Lichen and moss the lone stones greened,
    Green paths led lightly to its door,
Keen from her lair the spider leaned,
    And dusk to darkness wore.

Amidst the sedge a whisper ran,
    The West shut down a heavy eye,
And like last tapers, few and wan,
    The watch-stars kindled in the sky.


## Captain Lean

Out of the East a hurricane
    Swept down on Captain Lean –
That mariner and gentleman
    Will not again be seen.

He sailed his ship against the foes
    Of his own country dear,
But now in the trough of the billows
    An aimless course doth steer.

Powder was violets to his nostrils,
    Sweet the din of the fighting-line,
Now he is flotsam on the seas,
    And his bones are bleached with brine.

The stars move up along the sky,
    The moon she shines so bright,
And in that solitude the foam
    Sparkles unearthly white.

This is the tomb of Captain Lean,
    Would a straiter please his soul?
I trow he sleeps in peace,
    Howsoever the billows roll!

## The Raven's Tomb

'Build me my tomb,' the Raven said,
'Within the dark yew-tree,
So in the Autumn yewberries,
Sad lamps, may burn for me,
Summon the haunted beetle,
From twilight bud and bloom,
To drone a gloomy dirge for me
At dusk above my tomb.
Beseech ye too the glowworm
To rear her cloudy flame,
Where the small, flickering bats resort,
Whistling in tears my name.
Let the round dew a whisper make,
Welling on twig and thorn;
And only the grey cock at night
Call through his silver horn.
And you, dear sisters, don your black
For ever and a day,
To show how true a raven
In his tomb is laid away.'

## The Funeral

They dressed us up in black,
Susan and Tom and me;
And, walking through the fields
All beautiful to see,
With branches high in the air
And daisy and buttercup,

We heard the lark in the clouds, –
In black dressed up.

They took us to the graves,
Susan and Tom and me,
Where the long grasses grow
And the funeral tree:
We stood and watched; and the wind
Came softly out of the sky
And blew in Susan's hair,
As I stood close by.

Back through the fields we came,
Tom and Susan and me,
And we sat in the nursery together,
And had our tea.
And, looking out of the window,
I heard the thrushes sing;
But Tom fell asleep in his chair.
He was so tired, poor thing.

## Come!

From an island of the sea
Sounds a voice that summons me, –
'Turn thy prow, sailor, come
    With the wind home!'

Sweet o'er the rainbow foam,
Sweet in the treetops, 'Come,
Coral, cliff, and watery sand,
    Sea-wave to land!

'Droop not thy lids at night,
Furl not thy sails from flight! . . .'
Cease, cease, above the wave,
    Deep as the grave!

O, what voice of the salt sea
Calls me so insistently?
Echoes, echoes, night and day, –
    'Come, come away!'


## The Winter-Boy

I saw Jack Frost come louping o'er
    A hill of blinding snow;
And hooked upon his arm he bore
    A basket all aglow.

Cherries and damsons, peach and pear,
    The faint and moonlike quince;
Never before were fruits as rare,
    And never have been since.

'Come, will ye buy, ma'am?' says he sweet;
    And lo! began to fly
Flakes of bright, arrowy, frozen sleet
    From out the rosy sky.

'Silver nor pence, ma'am, ask I; but
    One kiss my cheek to warm, –
One with your scarlet lips tight shut
    Can do you, ma'am, no harm.'

O, and I stooped in that still place
   And pressed my lips to his;
And his cold locks about my face
   Shut darkness in my eyes.

Never, now never shall I be
   Lonely where snow is laid;
Sweet with his fruits comes louping he,
   And says the words he said.

His shrill voice echoes, slily creep
   His fingers cold and lean,
And lull my dazzled eyes asleep
   His icy locks between.


## They Told Me

They told me Pan was dead, but I
   Oft marvelled who it was that sang
Down the green valleys languidly
   Where the grey elder-thickets hang.

Sometimes I thought it was a bird
   My soul had charged with sorcery;
Sometimes it seemed my own heart heard
   Inland the sorrow of the sea.

But even where the primrose sets
   The seal of her pale loveliness,
I found amid the violets
   Tears of an antique bitterness.

# The Children of Stare

Winter is fallen early
  On the house of Stare;
Birds in reverberating flocks
  Haunt its ancestral box;
  Bright are the plenteous berries
  In clusters in the air.

Still is the fountain's music,
  The dark pool icy still,
Whereupon a small and sanguine sun
  Floats in a mirror on,
  Into a West of crimson,
  From a South of daffodil.

'Tis strange to see young children
  In such a wintry house;
Like rabbits' on the frozen snow
  Their tell-tale footprints go;
  Their laughter rings like timbrels
  'Neath evening ominous:

Their small and heightened faces
  Like wine-red winter buds;
Their frolic bodies gentle as
  Flakes in the air that pass,
  Frail as the twirling petal
  From the briar of the woods.

Above them silence lours,
  Still as an arctic sea;
Light fails; night falls; the wintry moon
  Glitters; the crocus soon

Will open grey and distracted
On earth's austerity:

Thick mystery, wild peril,
Law like an iron rod: –
Yet sport they on in Spring's attire,
Each with his tiny fire
Blown to a core of ardour
By the awful breath of God.


## The Birthnight: To F.

Dearest, it was a night
That in its darkness rocked Orion's stars;
A sighing wind ran faintly white
Along the willows, and the cedar boughs
Laid their wide hands in stealthy peace across
The starry silence of their antique moss:
No sound save rushing air
Cold, yet all sweet with Spring,
And in thy mother's arms, couched weeping there,
          Thou, lovely thing.


## Napoleon

'What is the world, O soldiers?
          It is I:
I, this incessant snow,
    This northern sky;
Soldiers, this solitude
    Through which we go
          is I.'

# Echo

'Who called?' I said, and the words
    Through the whispering glades,
Hither, thither, baffled the birds –
    'Who called? Who called?'

The leafy boughs on high
    Hissed in the sun;
The dark air carried my cry
    Faintingly on:

Eyes in the green, in the shade,
    In the motionless brake,
Voices that said what I said,
    For mockery's sake:

'Who cares?' I bawled through my tears;
    The wind fell low:
In the silence, 'Who cares? Who cares?'
    Wailed to and fro.


# Autumn

There is a wind where the rose was;
Cold rain where sweet grass was;
    And clouds like sheep
    Stream o'er the steep
Grey skies where the lark was.

Nought gold where your hair was;
Nought warm where your hand was;

But phantom, forlorn,
Beneath the thorn,
Your ghost where your face was.

Sad winds where your voice was;
Tears, tears where my heart was;
And ever with me,
Child, ever with me,
Silence where hope was.


## The Scarecrow

All winter through I bow my head
Beneath the driving rain;
The North Wind powders me with snow
And blows me black again;
At midnight in a maze of stars
I flame with glittering rime,
And stand, above the stubble, stiff
As mail at morning-prime.
But when that child, called Spring, and all
His host of children, come,
Scattering their buds and dew upon
These acres of my home,
Some rapture in my rags awakes;
I lift void eyes and scan
The skies for crows, those ravening foes,
Of my strange master, Man.
I watch him striding lank behind
His clashing team, and know
Soon will the wheat swish body high
Where once lay sterile snow;

Soon shall I gaze across a sea
    Of sun-begotten grain,
Which my unflinching watch hath sealed
    For harvest once again.


## Nod

Softly along the road of evening,
    In a twilight dim with rose,
Wrinkled with age, and drenched with dew,
    Old Nod, the shepherd, goes.

His drowsy flock streams on before him,
    Their fleeces charged with gold,
To where the sun's last beam leans low
    On Nod the shepherd's fold.

The hedge is quick and green with brier,
    From their sand the conies creep;
And all the birds that fly in heaven
    Flock singing home to sleep.

His lambs outnumber a noon's roses,
    Yet, when night's shadows fall,
His blind old sheep-dog, Slumber-soon,
    Misses not one of all.

His are the quiet steeps of dreamland,
    The waters of no-more-pain,
His ram's bell rings 'neath an arch of stars,
    'Rest, rest and rest again.'

# Winter

Clouded with snow
  The bleak winds blow,
And shrill on leafless bough
The robin with its burning breast
  Alone sings now.

The rayless sun,
  Day's journey done,
Sheds its last ebbing light
On fields in leagues of beauty spread
  Unearthly white.

Thick draws the dark,
  And spark by spark,
The frost-fires kindle, and soon
Over that sea of frozen foam
  Floats the white moon.


# All That's Past

Very old are the woods;
  And the buds that break
Out of the brier's boughs,
  When March winds wake,
So old with their beauty are –
  Oh, no man knows
Through what wild centuries
  Roves back the rose.

Very old are the brooks;
  And the rills that rise

Where snow sleeps cold beneath
    The azure skies
Sing such a history
    Of come and gone,
Their every drop is as wise
    As Solomon.

Very old are we men;
    Our dreams are tales
Told in dim Eden
    By Eve's nightingales;
We wake and whisper awhile,
    But, the day gone by,
Silence and sleep like fields
    Of amaranth lie.


## Never More, Sailor

Never more, Sailor,
Shalt thou be
Tossed on the wind-ridden,
Restless sea.
Its tides may labour;
All the world
Shake 'neath that weight
Of waters hurled:
But its whole shock
Can only stir
Thy dust to a quiet
Even quieter.
Thou mock'st at land
Who now art come

To such a small
And shallow home;
Yet bore the sea
Full many a care
For bones that once
A sailor's were.
And though the grave's
Deep soundlessness
Thy once sea-deafened
Ear distress,
No robin ever
On the deep
Hopped with his song
To haunt thy sleep.


Arabia

Far are the shades of Arabia,
    Where the Princes ride at noon,
'Mid the verdurous vales and thickets,
    Under the ghost of the moon;
And so dark is that vaulted purple
    Flowers in the forest rise
And toss into blossom 'gainst the phantom stars
    Pale in the noonday skies.

Sweet is the music of Arabia
    In my heart, when out of dreams
I still in the thin clear mirk of dawn
    Descry her gliding streams;
Hear her strange lutes on the green banks
    Ring loud with the grief and delight

Of the dim-silked, dark-haired Musicians
  In the brooding silence of night.

They haunt me – her lutes and her forests;
  No beauty on earth I see
But shadowed with that dream recalls
  Her loveliness to me:
Still eyes look coldly upon me,
  Cold voices whisper and say –
'He is crazed with the spell of far Arabia,
  They have stolen his wits away.'


## Never-to-Be

Down by the waters of the sea
Reigns the King of Never-to-be.
His palace walls are black with night;
His torches star and moon's light,
And for his timepiece deep and grave
Beats on the green unhastening wave.

Windswept are his high corridors;
His pleasance the sea-mantled shores;
For sentinel a shadow stands
With hair in heaven, and cloudy hands;
And round his bed, king's guards to be,
Watch pines in iron solemnity.

His hound is mute; his steed at will
Roams pastures deep with asphodel;
His queen is to her slumber gone;
His courtiers mute lie, hewn in stone;
He hath forgot where he did hide
His sceptre in the mountain-side.

Grey-capped and muttering, mad is he –
The childless King of Never-to-be;
For all his people in the deep
Keep, everlasting, fast asleep;
And all his realm is foam and rain,
Whispering of what comes not again.


## The Listeners

'Is there anybody there?' said the Traveller,
    Knocking on the moonlit door;
And his horse in the silence champed the grasses
    Of the forest's ferny floor:
And a bird flew up out of the turret,
    Above the Traveller's head:
And he smote upon the door again a second time;
    'Is there anybody there?' he said.
But no one descended to the Traveller;
    No head from the leaf-fringed sill
Leaned over and looked into his grey eyes,
    Where he stood perplexed and still.
But only a host of phantom listeners
    That dwelt in the lone house then
Stood listening in the quiet of the moonlight
    To that voice from the world of men:
Stood thronging the faint moonbeams on the dark stair,
    That goes down to the empty hall,
Hearkening in an air stirred and shaken
    By the lonely Traveller's call.
And he felt in his heart their strangeness,
    Their stillness answering his cry,
While his horse moved, cropping the dark turf,

'Neath the starred and leafy sky;
For he suddenly smote on the door, even
    Louder, and lifted his head: –
'Tell them I came, and no one answered,
    That I kept my word,' he said.
Never the least stir made the listeners,
    Though every word he spake
Fell echoing through the shadowiness of the still house
    From the one man left awake:
Ay, they heard his foot upon the stirrup,
    And the sound of iron on stone,
And how the silence surged softly backward,
    When the plunging hoofs were gone.


## Winter Dusk

Dark frost was in the air without,
    The dusk was still with cold and gloom,
When less than even a shadow came
        And stood within the room.

But of the three around the fire,
    None turned a questioning head to look,
Still read a clear voice, on and on,
        Still stooped they o'er their book.

The children watched their mother's eyes
    Moving on softly line to line;
It seemed to listen too – that shade,
        Yet made no outward sign.

The fire-flames crooned a tiny song,
 No cold wind stirred the wintry tree;
The children both in Faërie dreamed
  Beside their mother's knee.

And nearer yet that spirit drew
 Above that heedless one, intent
Only on what the simple words
  Of her small story meant.

No voiceless sorrow grieved her mind,
 No memory her bosom stirred,
Nor dreamed she, as she read to two,
  'Twas surely three who heard.

Yet when, the story done, she smiled
 From face to face, serene and clear,
A love, half dread, sprang up, as she
  Leaned close and drew them near


## An Epitaph

Here lies a most beautiful lady,
Light of step and heart was she;
I think she was the most beautiful lady
That ever was in the West Country.

But beauty vanishes; beauty passes;
However rare – rare it be;
And when I crumble, who will remember
This lady of the West Country?

## Alas, Alack!

Ann, Ann!
   Come! quick as you can!
There's a fish that *talks*
   In the frying-pan.
Out of the fat,
   As clear as glass,
He put up his mouth
   And moaned 'Alas!'
Oh, most mournful,
   'Alas, alack!'
Then turned to his sizzling,
   And sank him back.


## The Huntsmen

Three jolly gentlemen,
   In coats of red,
Rode their horses
   Up to bed.

Three jolly gentlemen
   Snored till morn,
Their horses champing
   The golden corn.

Three jolly gentlemen,
   At break of day,
Came clitter-clatter down the stairs
   And galloped away.

## Some One

Some one came knocking
    At my wee, small door;
Some one came knocking,
    I'm sure – sure – sure;
I listened, I opened,
    I looked to left and right,
But nought there was a-stirring
    In the still dark night;
Only the busy beetle
    Tap-tapping in the wall,
Only from the forest
    The screech-owl's call,
Only the cricket whistling
    While the dewdrops fall,
So I know not who came knocking,
    At all, at all, at all.

## Old Shellover

'Come!' said Old Shellover.
'What?' says Creep.
'The horny old Gardener's fast asleep;
The fat cock Thrush
To his nest has gone;
And the dew shines bright
In the rising Moon;
Old Sallie Worm from her hole doth peep:
Come!' said Old Shellover.
'Ay!' said Creep.

# Jim Jay

Do diddle di do,
   Poor Jim Jay
Got stuck fast
   In Yesterday.
Squinting he was,
   On cross-legs bent,
Never heeding
   The wind was spent.
Round veered the weathercock,
   The sun drew in –
And stuck was Jim
   Like a rusty pin . . .
We pulled and we pulled
   From seven till twelve,
Jim, too frightened
   To help himself.
But all in vain.
   The clock struck one,
And there was Jim
   A little bit gone.
At half-past five
   You scarce could see
A glimpse of his flapping
   Handkerchee.
And when came noon,
   And we climbed sky-high,
Jim was a speck
   Slip – slipping by.
Come to-morrow,
   The neighbours say,

He'll be past crying for:
    Poor Jim Jay.


## Miss T.

It's a very odd thing –
    As odd as can be –
That whatever Miss T. eats
    Turns into Miss T.;
Porridge and apples,
    Mince, muffins and mutton,
Jam, junket, jumbles –
    Not a rap, not a button
It matters; the moment
    They're out of her plate,
Though shared by Miss Butcher
    And sour Mr. Bate;
Tiny and cheerful,
    And neat as can be,
Whatever Miss T. eats
    Turns into Miss T.


## Mistletoe

Sitting under the mistletoe
(Pale-green, fairy mistletoe),
One last candle burning low,
All the sleepy dancers gone,
Just one candle burning on,
Shadows lurking everywhere:
Some one came, and kissed me there.

Tired I was; my head would go
Nodding under the mistletoe
(Pale-green, fairy mistletoe);
No footsteps came, no voice, but only,
Just as I sat there, sleepy, lonely,
Stooped in the still and shadowy air
Lips unseen – and kissed me there.


## The Lost Shoe

Poor little Lucy
    By some mischance,
Lost her shoe
    As she did dance:
'Twas not on the stairs,
    Not in the hall;
Not where they sat
    At supper at all.
She looked in the garden,
    But there it was not;
Henhouse, or kennel,
    Or high dovecote.
Dairy and meadow,
    And wild woods through
Showed not a trace
    Of Lucy's shoe.
Bird nor bunny
    Nor glimmering moon
Breathed a whisper
    Of where 'twas gone.
It was cried and cried,
    *Oyez* and *Oyez!*

In French, Dutch, Latin
    And Portuguese.
Ships the dark seas
    Went plunging through,
But none brought news
    Of Lucy's shoe;
And still she patters,
    In silk and leather,
Snow, sand, shingle,
    In every weather;
Spain, and Africa,
    Hindustan,
Java, China,
    And lamped Japan,
Plain and desert,
    She hops – hops through,
Pernambuco
    To gold Peru;
Mountain and forest,
    And river too,
All the world over
    For her lost shoe.


## The Sea Boy

Peter went – and nobody there –
Down by the sandy sea,
And he danced a jig, while the moon shone big,
All in his lone danced he;
And the surf splashed over his tippeting toes,
And he sang his riddle-cum-ree,
With hair a-dangling,

Moon a-spangling
The bubbles and froth of the sea.
He danced him to, and he danced him fro,
And he twirled himself about,
And now the starry waves tossed in,
And now the waves washed out;
Bare as an acorn, bare as a nut,
Nose and toes and knee,
Peter the sea-boy danced and pranced,
And sang his riddle-cum-ree.


## Off the Ground

Three jolly Farmers
Once bet a pound
Each dance the others would
Off the ground.
Out of their coats
They slipped right soon,
And neat and nicesome,
Put each his shoon.

One – Two – Three! –
And away they go,
Not too fast,
And not too slow;
Out from the elm-tree's
Noonday shadow,
Into the sun
And across the meadow.
Past the schoolroom,
With knees well bent

Fingers a-flicking,
They dancing went.
Up sides and over,
And round and round,
They crossed click-clacking,
The Parish bound.
By Tupman's meadow
They did their mile,
Tee-to-tum
On a three-barred stile.
Then straight through Whipham,
Downhill to Week,
Footing it lightsome,
But not too quick,
Up fields to Watchet,
And on through Wye,
Till seven fine churches
They'd seen skip by –
Seven fine churches,
And five old mills,
Farms in the valley,
And sheep on the hills;
Old Man's Acre
And Dead Man's Pool
All left behind,
As they danced through Wool.

And Wool gone by,
Like tops that seem
To spin in sleep
They danced in dream:
Withy – Wellover –
Wassop – Wo –

Like an old clock
Their heels did go.
A league and a league
And a league they went,
And not one weary,
And not one spent.
And lo, and behold!
Past Willow-cum-Leigh
Stretched with its waters
The great green sea.

Says Farmer Bates,
'I puffs and I blows,
What's under the water,
Why, no man knows!'
Says Farmer Giles,
'My wind comes weak,
And a good man drownded
Is far to seek.'
But Farmer Turvey,
On twirling toes
Up's with his gaiters,
And in he goes:
Down where the mermaids
Pluck and play
On their twangling harps
In a sea-green day;
Down where the mermaids,
Finned and fair,
Sleek with their combs
Their yellow hair. . . .

Bates and Giles –
On the shingle sat,
Gazing at Turvey's
Floating hat.
But never a ripple
Nor bubble told
Where he was supping
Off plates of gold.
Never an echo
Rilled through the sea
Of the feasting and dancing
And minstrelsy.
They called – called – called:
Came no reply:
Nought but the ripples'
Sandy sigh.
Then glum and silent
They sat instead,
Vacantly brooding
On home and bed,
Till both together
Stood up and said: –
'Us knows not, dreams not,
Where you be,
Turvey, unless
In the deep blue sea;
But axcusing silver –
And it comes most willing –
Here's us two paying
Our forty shilling;
For it's sartin sure, Turvey,
Safe and sound,
You danced us square, Turvey;
Off the ground!'

# Late

Three small men in a small house,
　　And none to hear them say,
'One for his nob,' and 'One for his noddle,'
　　And 'One for his dumb dog Stray!'
'Clubs are trumps – and he's dealt and bluffed':
　　'And Jack of diamonds led':
'And perhaps the cullie has dropped a shoe;
　　He tarries so late,' they said,

Three small men in a small house,
　　And one small empty chair,
One with his moleskin over his brows,
　　One with his crany bare,
And one with a dismal cast in his eye,
　　Rocking a heavy head . . .
'And perhaps the cullie's at *The Wide World's End*;
　　He tarries so late' they said.

Three small men in a small house,
　　And a candle guttering low,
One with his cheek on the ace of spades,
　　And two on the boards below.
And a window black 'gainst a waste of stars,
　　And a moon five dark nights dead . . .
'Who's that a-knocking and a-knocking and a-knocking?'
　　One stirred in his sleep and said.

## King David

King David was a sorrowful man:
  No cause for his sorrow had he:
And he called for the music of a hundred harps,
  To solace his melancholy.

They played till they all fell silent:
  Played – and play sweet did they;
But the sorrow that haunted the heart of King David
  They could not charm away.

He rose; and in his garden
  Walked by the moon alone,
A nightingale hidden in a cypress-tree
  Jargoned on and on.

King David lifted his sad eyes
  Into the dark-boughed tree –
'Tell me, thou little bird that singest,
  Who taught my grief to thee?'

But the bird in no wise heeded;
  And the king in the cool of the moon
Hearkened to the nightingale's sorrowfulness,
  Till all his own was gone.


## Nicholas Nye

Thistle and darnel and dock grew there,
  And a bush, in the corner, of may,
On the orchard wall I used to sprawl
  In the blazing heat of the day;

Half asleep and half awake,
    While the birds went twittering by,
And nobody there my lone to share
        But Nicholas Nye.

Nicholas Nye was lean and grey,
    Lame of a leg and old,
More than a score of donkey's years
    He had seen since he was foaled;
He munched the thistles, purple and spiked,
    Would sometimes stoop and sigh,
And turn his head, as if he said,
        'Poor Nicholas Nye!'

Alone with his shadow he'd drowse in the meadow,
    Lazily swinging his tail,
At break of day he used to bray, –
    Not much too hearty and hale;
But a wonderful gumption was under his skin,
    And a clear calm light in his eye,
And once in a while: he'd smile . . .
        Would Nicholas Nye.

Seem to be smiling at me, he would,
    From his bush in the corner, of may, –
Bony and ownerless, widowed and worn,
    Knobble-kneed, lonely and grey;
And over the grass would seem to pass
    'Neath the deep dark blue of the sky,
Something much better than words between me
        And Nicholas Nye.

But dusk would come in the apple boughs,
    The green of the glow-worm shine,
The birds in nest would crouch to rest,

And home I'd trudge to mine;
And there, in the moonlight, dark with dew
    Asking not wherefore nor why,
Would brood like a ghost, and as still as a post,
    Old Nicholas Nye.


## The Pigs and the Charcoal-Burner

The old Pig said to the little pigs,
    'In the forest is truffles and mast,
Follow me then, all ye little pigs,
    Follow me fast!'

The Charcoal-burner sat in the shade,
    His chin on his thumb,
And saw the big Pig and the little pigs,
    Chuffling come.

He watched 'neath a green and giant bough,
    And the pigs in the ground
Made a wonderful grizzling and gruzzling
    And greedy sound.

And when, full-fed, they were gone, and Night
    Walked her starry ways,
He stared with his cheeks in his hands
    At his sullen blaze.


## Five Eyes

In Hans' old Mill his three black cats
Watch his bins for the thieving rats.

Whisker and claw, they crouch in the night,
Their five eyes smouldering green and bright
Squeaks from the flour sacks, squeaks from where
The cold wind stirs on the empty stair,
Squeaking and scampering, everywhere.
Then down they pounce, now in, now out,
At whisking tail, and sniffing snout;
While lean old Hans he snores away
Till peep of light at break of day;
Then up he climbs to his creaking mill,
Out come his cats all grey with meal –
Jekkel, and Jessup, and one-eyed Jill.


## The Old Stone House

Nothing on the grey roof, nothing on the brown,
Only a little greening where the rain drips down;
Nobody at the window, nobody at the door,
Only a little hollow which a foot once wore;
But still I tread on tiptoe, still tiptoe on I go,
Past nettles, porch, and weedy well, for oh, I know
A friendless face is peering, and a clear still eye
Peeps closely through the casement as my step goes by.


## The Changeling

'Ahoy, and ahoy!'
    'Twixt mocking and merry –
'Ahoy and ahoy, there,
    Young man of the ferry!'

She stood on the steps
    In the watery gloom –
That Changeling – 'Ahoy, there!'
    She called him to come.
He came on the green wave,
    He came on the grey,
Where stooped that sweet lady
    That still summer's day.
He fell in a dream
    Of her beautiful face,
As she sat on the thwart
    And smiled in her place.
No echo his oar woke,
    Float silent did they,
Past low-grazing cattle
    In the sweet of the hay.
And still in a dream
    At her beauty sat he,
Drifting stern foremost
    Down – down to the sea.
Come you, then: call,
    When the twilight apace
Brings shadow to brood
    On the loveliest face;
You shall hear o'er the water
    Ring faint in the grey –
'Ahoy, and ahoy, there!'
    And tremble away;
'Ahoy, and ahoy! . . .'
    And tremble away.

# Bewitched

I have heard a lady this night,
   Lissome and jimp and slim,
Calling me – calling me over the heather,
   'Neath the beech boughs dusk and dim.

I have followed a lady this night,
   Followed her far and lone,
Fox and adder and weasel know
   The ways that we have gone.

I sit at my supper 'mid honest faces,
   And crumble my crust and say
Nought in the long-drawn drawl of the voices
   Talking the hours away.

I'll go to my chamber under the gable,
   And the moon will lift her light
In at my lattice from over the moorland
   Hollow and still and bright.

And I know she will shine on a lady of witchcraft,
   Gladness and grief to see,
Who has taken my heart with her nimble fingers,
   Calls in my dreams to me;

Who has led me a dance by dell and dingle
   My human soul to win,
Made me a changeling to my own, own mother,
   A stranger to my kin.

# Silver

Slowly, silently, now the moon
Walks the night in her silver shoon;
This way, and that, she peers, and sees
Silver fruit upon silver trees;
One by one the casements catch
Her beams beneath the silvery thatch;
Couched in his kennel, like a log,
With paws of silver sleeps the dog;
From their shadowy cote the white breasts peep
Of doves in a silver-feathered sleep;
A harvest mouse goes scampering by,
With silver claws, and silver eye;
And moveless fish in the water gleam,
By silver reeds in a silver stream.


# The Song of Soldiers

As I sat musing by the frozen dyke,
There was one man marching with a bright steel pike,
Marching in the dayshine like a ghost came he,
And behind me was the moaning and the murmur of the sea.

As I sat musing, 'twas not one but ten –
Rank on rank of ghostly soldiers marching o'er the fen,
Marching in the misty air they showed in dreams to me,
And behind me was the shouting and the shattering of
    the sea.

As I sat musing, 'twas a host in dark array,
With their horses and their cannon wheeling onward to the
    fray,
Moving like a shadow to the fate the brave must dree,
And behind me roared the drums, rang the trumpets of
    the sea.


## A Song of Enchantment

A Song of Enchantment I sang me there,
In a green – green wood, by waters fair,
Just as the words came up to me
I sang it under the wild wood tree.

Widdershins turned I, singing it low,
Watching the wild birds come and go;
No cloud in the deep dark blue to be seen
Under the thick-thatched branches green.

Twilight came; silence came;
The planet of evening's silver flame;
By darkening paths I wandered through
Thickets trembling with drops of dew.

But the music is lost and the words are gone
Of the song I sang as I sat alone,
Ages and ages have fallen on me –
On the wood and the pool and the elder tree.

# Dream-Song

Sunlight, moonlight,
Twilight, starlight –
Gloaming at the close of day,
And an owl calling,
Cool dews falling
In a wood of oak and may.

Lantern-light, taper-light,
Torchlight, no-light:
Darkness at the shut of day,
And lions roaring,
Their wrath pouring
In wild waste places far away.

Elf-light, bat-light,
Touchwood-light and toad-light,
And the sea a shimmering gloom of grey,
And a small face smiling
In a dream's beguiling
In a world of wonders far away.


# The Song of the Mad Prince

Who said, 'Peacock Pie'?
    The old King to the sparrow:
Who said, 'Crops are ripe'?
    Rust to the harrow:
Who said, 'Where sleeps she now?
    Where rests she now her head,
Bathed in eve's loveliness'? –
    That's what I said.

Who said, 'Ay, mum's the word'?
    Sexton to willow:
Who said, 'Green dusk for dreams,
    Moss for a pillow'?
Who said, 'All Time's delight
    Hath she for narrow bed;
Life's troubled bubble broken'? –
    That's what I said.


## Alone

The abode of the nightingale is bare,
Flowered frost congeals in the gelid air,
The fox howls from his frozen lair:
        Alas, my loved one is gone,
        I am alone;
        It is winter.

Once the pink cast a winy smell,
The wild bee hung in the hyacinth bell,
Light in effulgence of beauty fell:
        Alas, my loved one is gone,
        I am alone;
        It is winter.

My candle a silent fire doth shed,
Starry Orion hunts o'erhead;
Come moth, come shadow, the world is dead:
        Alas, my loved one is gone,
        I am alone;
        It is winter.

# Mistress Fell

'Whom seek you here, sweet Mistress Fell?'
'One who loved me passing well.
Dark his eye, wild his face –
Stranger, if in this lonely place
Bide such an one, then, prythee, say
*I* am come here to-day.'

'Many his like, Mistress Fell?'
'I did not look, so cannot tell.
Only this I surely know,
When his voice called me, I must go;
Touched me his fingers, and my heart
Leapt at the sweet pain's smart.'

'Why did he leave you, Mistress Fell?'
'Magic laid its dreary spell –
Stranger, he was fast asleep;
Into his dream I tried to creep;
Called his name, soft was my cry;
He answered – not one sigh.

'The flower and the thorn are here;
Falleth the night-dew, cold and clear;
Out of her bower the bird replies,
Mocking the dark with ecstasies,
See how the earth's green grass doth grow,
Praising what sleeps below!

'Thus have they told me. And I come,
As flies the wounded wild-bird home.
Not tears I give; but all that he
Clasped in his arms, sweet charity;
All that he loved – to him I bring
For a close whispering.'


## The Ghost

'Who knocks?' 'I, who was beautiful,
   Beyond all dreams to restore,
I, from the roots of the dark thorn am hither.
   And knock on the door.'

'Who speaks?' 'I – once was my speech
   Sweet as the bird's on the air,
When echo lurks by the waters to heed;
   'Tis I speak thee fair.'

'Dark is the hour!' 'Ay, and cold.'
   'Lone is my house.' 'Ah, but mine?'
'Sight, touch, lips, eyes yearned in vain.'
   'Long dead these to thine . . .'

Silence. Still faint on the porch
   Brake the flames of the stars.
In gloom groped a hope-wearied hand
   Over keys, bolts, and bars.

A face peered. All the grey night
   In chaos of vacancy shone;
Nought but vast sorrow was there –
   The sweet cheat gone.

# The Stranger

In the woods as I did walk,
    Dappled with the moon's beam,
I did with a Stranger talk,
    And his name was Dream.

Spurred his heel, dark his cloak,
    Shady-wide his bonnet's brim;
His horse beneath a silvery oak
    Grazed as I talked with him.

Softly his breast-brooch burned and shone;
    Hill and deep were in his eyes;
One of his hands held mine, and one
    The fruit that makes men wise.

Wondrously strange was earth to see,
    Flowers white as milk did gleam;
Spread to Heaven the Assyrian Tree,
    Over my head with Dream.

Dews were still betwixt us twain;
    Stars a trembling beauty shed;
Yet, not a whisper comes again
    Of the words he said.

# The Marionettes

Let the foul Scene proceed:
    There's laughter in the wings;
'Tis sawdust that they bleed,
    Only a box Death brings.

How rare a skill is theirs –
    These extreme pangs to show.
How real a frenzy wears
    Each feigner of woe!

Gigantic dins uprise!
    Even the gods must feel
A smarting of the eyes
    As these fumes upsweel.

Strange, such a Piece is free.
    While we Spectators sit,
Aghast at its agony,
    Yet absorbed in it!

Dark is the outer air,
    Coldly the night draughts blow,
Mutely we stare, and stare
    At the frenzied Show.

Yet heaven hath its quiet shroud
    Of deep, immutable blue –
We cry 'An end!' We are bowed
    By the dread, 'It's true!'

While the Shape who hoofs applause
    Behind our deafened ear,
Hoots – angel-wise – 'the Cause!'
    And affrights even fear.

# The Three Strangers

Far are those tranquil hills,
　　Dyed with fair evening's rose;
On urgent, secret errand bent,
　　　A traveller goes.

Approach him strangers three,
　　Barefooted, cowled; their eyes
Scan the lone, hastening solitary
　　　With dumb surmise.

One instant in close speech
　　With them he doth confer:
God-sped, he hasteneth on,
　　　That anxious traveller . . .

I was that man – in a dream:
　　And each world's night in vain
I patient wait on sleep to unveil
　　　Those vivid hills again.

Would that they three could know
　　How yet burns on in me
Love – from one lost in Paradise –
　　　For their grave courtesy.


# The Scribe

What lovely things
　　Thy hand hath made:
The smooth-plumed bird
　　In its emerald shade.

The seed of the grass,
   The speck of stone
Which the wayfaring ant
   Stirs – and hastes on!

Though I should sit
   By some tarn in thy hills,
Using its ink
   As the spirit wills
To write of Earth's wonders,
   Its live, willed things,
Flit would the ages
   On soundless wings
Ere unto Z
   My pen drew nigh;
Leviathan told,
   And the honey-fly:
And still would remain
   My wit to try –
My worn reeds broken,
   The dark tarn dry,
All words forgotten –
   Thou, Lord, and I.


Fare Well

When I lie where shades of darkness
Shall no more assail mine eyes,
Nor the rain make lamentation
      When the wind sighs;

How will fare the world whose wonder
Was the very proof of me?
Memory fades, must the remembered
Perishing be?

Oh, when this my dust surrenders
Hand, foot, lip, to dust again,
May these loved and loving faces
Please other men!
May the rusting harvest hedgerow
Still the Traveller's Joy entwine,
And as happy children gather
Posies once mine.

Look thy last on all things lovely,
Every hour. Let no night
Seal thy sense in deathly slumber
Till to delight
Thou have paid thy utmost blessing;
Since that all things thou wouldst praise
Beauty took from those who loved them
In other days.


## The Comb

My mother sate me at her glass;
This necklet of bright flowers she wove;
Crisscross her gentle hands did pass,
And wound in my hair her love.

Deep in the mirror our glances met,
And grieved, lest from her care I roam,
She kissed me through her tears, and set
On high this spangling comb.

## The Moth

Isled in the midnight air,
Musked with the dark's faint bloom,
Out into glooming and secret haunts
    The flame cries, 'Come!'

Lovely in dye and fan,
A-tremble in shimmering grace,
A moth from her winter swoon
    Uplifts her face:

Stares from her glamorous eyes;
Wafts her on plumes like mist;
In ecstasy swirls and sways
    To her strange tryst.


## Titmouse

If you would happy company win,
Dangle a palm-nut from a tree,
Idly in green to sway and spin,
Its snow-pulped kernel for bait; and see
    A nimble titmouse enter in.

Out of earth's vast unknown of air,
Out of all summer, from wave to wave,
He'll perch, and prank his feathers fair,
Jangle a glass-clear wildering stave,
    And take his commons there –

This tiny son of life; this spright,
By momentary Human sought,
Plume will his wing in the dappling light,
Clash timbrel shrill and gay –
And into Time's enormous Nought,
    Sweet-fed, will flit away.


## The Veil

I think and think; yet still I fail –
Why does this lady wear a veil?
Why thus elect to mask her face
Beneath that dainty web of lace?
The tip of a small nose I see,
And two red lips, set curiously
Like twin-born cherries on one stem,
And yet she has netted even them.
Her eyes, it's plain, survey with ease
All that to glance upon they please.
Yet, whether hazel, grey, or blue,
Or that even lovelier lilac hue,
I cannot guess: why – why deny
Such beauty to the passer-by?
Out of a bush a nightingale
May expound his song; beneath that veil
A happy mouth no doubt can make
English sound sweeter for its sake.
But then, why muffle in, like this,
What every blossomy wind would kiss?
Why in that little night disguise
A daylight face, those starry eyes?

## The Suicide

Did these night-hung houses,
Of quiet, starlit stone,
Breathe not a whisper – 'Stay,
Thou unhappy one;
Whither so secret away?'

Sighed not the unfriending wind,
Chill with nocturnal dew,
'Pause, pause, in thy haste,
O thou distraught! I too
Tryst with the Atlantic waste.'

Steep fell the drowsy street;
In slumber the world was blind:
Breathed not one midnight flower
Peace in thy broken mind? –
'Brief, yet sweet, is life's hour.'

Syllabled thy last tide –
By as dark moon stirred,
And doomed to forlorn unrest –
Not one compassionate word? . . .
'Cold is this breast.'


## Good-Bye

The last of last words spoken is, Good-bye –
The last dismantled flower in the weed-grown hedge,
The last thin rumour of a feeble bell far ringing,
The last blind rat to spurn the mildewed rye.

A hardening darkness glasses the haunted eye,
Shines into nothing the watcher's burnt-out candle,
Wreathes into scentless nothing the wasting incense,
Faints in the outer silence the hunting-cry.

Love of its muted music breathes no sigh,
Thought in her ivory tower gropes in her spinning,
Toss on in vain the whispering trees of Eden,
Last of all last words spoken is, Good-bye.


## The Corner Stone

Sterile these stones
By time in ruin laid.
Yet many a creeping thing
Its haven has made
In these least crannies, where falls
Dark's dew, and noonday shade.

The claw of the tender bird
Finds lodgement here;
Dye-winged butterflies poise;
Emmet and beetle steer
Their busy course; the bee
Drones, laden, near.

Their myriad-mirrored eyes
Great day reflect.
By their exquisite farings
Is this granite specked;
Is trodden to infinite dust;
By gnawing lichens decked.

Toward what eventual dream
Sleeps its cold on,
When into ultimate dark
These lives shall be gone,
And even of man not a shadow remain
Of all he has done?


## The Familiar

'Are you far away?'
'Yea, I am far – far;
Where the green wave shelves to the sand,
And the rainbows are;
And an ageless sun beats fierce
From an empty sky:
There, O thou Shadow forlorn,
Is the wraith of thee, I.'

'Are you happy, most Lone?'
'Happy, forsooth!
Who am eyes of the air; the voice of the foam;
Ah, happy in truth.
My hair is astream, this cheek
Glistens like silver, and see,
As the gold to the dross, the ghost in the mirk,
I am calling to thee.'

'Nay, I am bound.
And your cry faints out in your mind.
Peace not on earth have I found,
Yet to earth am resigned.
Cease thy shrill mockery, Voice,
Nor answer again.'

'O Master, thick cloud shuts thee out
And cold tempests of rain.'


## Sunk Lyonesse

In sea-cold Lyonesse,
When the Sabbath eve shafts down
On the roofs, walls, belfries
Of the foundered town,
The Nereids pluck their lyres
Where the green translucency beats,
And with motionless eyes at gaze
Make minstrelsy in the streets.

And the ocean water stirs
In salt-worn casemate and porch.
Plies the blunt-snouted fish
With fire in his skull for torch.
And the ringing wires resound;
And the unearthly lovely weep,
In lament of the music they make
In the sullen courts of sleep:
Whose marble flowers bloom for aye:
And – lapped by the moon-guiled tide –
Mock their carver with heart of stone,
Caged in his stone-ribbed side.


## Who?

1st Stranger:    Who walks with us on the hills?
2nd Stranger:    I cannot see for the mist.

| 3rd Stranger: | Running water I hear, |
| | Keeping lugubrious tryst |
| | With its cresses and grasses and weeds, |
| | In the white obscure light from the sky. |
| 2nd Stranger: | *Who walks with us on the hills?* |
| Wild Bird: | *Ay! . . . Aye! . . . Ay! . . .* |

## Bitter Waters

In a dense wood, a drear wood,
   Dark water is flowing;
Deep, deep, beyond sounding,
   A flood ever flowing.

There harbours no wild bird,
   No wanderer stays there;
Wreathed in mist, sheds pale Ishtar
   Her sorrowful rays there.

Take thy net; cast thy line;
   Manna sweet be thy baiting;
Time's desolate ages
   Shall still find thee waiting

For quick fish to rise there,
   Or butterfly wooing,
Or flower's honeyed beauty,
   Or wood-pigeon cooing.

Inland wellsprings are sweet;
   But to lips, parched and dry,
Salt, salt is the savour
   Of these; faint their sigh.

Bitter Babylon's waters.
   Zion, distant and fair.
We hanged up our harps
   On the trees that are there.


## Crazed

I know a pool where nightshade preens
Her poisonous fruitage in the moon;
Where the frail aspen her shadow leans
In midnight cold a-swoon.

I know a meadow flat with gold –
A million million burning flowers
In moon-sun's thirst their buds unfold
Beneath his blazing showers.

I saw a crazèd face, did I,
Stare from the lattice of a mill,
While the lank sails clacked idly by
High on the windy hill.


## Nat Vole

Here lieth Nat Vole,
Asleep now, poor Soul!
'Twas one of his whims
To be telling his dreams,
Of the Lands therein seen
And the Journeys he'd been!
La, if now he could speak,
He'd not listeners seek!

## John Virgin

If thou, Stranger, be John Virgin, then the
Corse withinunder is nameless, for the Sea
  so disfigured thy Face, none could tell
  whether thou were John Virgin or no:
    Ay, and whatever name I bore
     I thank the Lord I be
    Six foot in English earth, and not
     Six fathom in the sea.


## Chrystopher Orcherdson

Here restes ye boddie of one
Chrystopher Orcherdson.
Lyf he lived merrilie;
Nowe he doth deathlie lie:
All ye joye from his brighte face
Quencht in this bitter place.
With gratefull voice then saye,
Not oures, but Goddes waye!


## Richard Halladay

Each in place as God did 'gree
Here lie all ye Bones of me.
But what made them walke up right,
And, cladde in Flesh, a goodly Sight,
One of hostes of Living Men –
    Ask again – ask again!

## Thomas Logge

Here lies Thomas Logge  –  A Rascally Dogge;
A poor useless creature  –  by choice as by nature;
Who never served God  –  for kindness or Rod;
Who, for pleasure or penny,  –  never did any
Work in his life  –  but to marry a Wife,
And live aye in strife:
And all this he says  –  at the end of his days
Lest some fine canting pen
Should be at him again.


## O Passer-By, Beware!

O passer-by, beware!
Is the day fair?  –
Yet unto evening shall the day spin on
And soon thy sun be gone;
Then darkness come,
And this, a narrow home.
Not that I bid thee fear:
Only, when thou at last lie here,
Bethink thee, there shall surely be
    Thy Self for company.


## The Shubble

There was an old man said, 'I fear
That life, my dear friends, is a bubble,
Still, with all due respect to a Philistine ear,

[68]

A limerick's best when it's double.'
When they said, 'But the waste
    Of time, temper, taste!'
He gulped down his ink with cantankerous haste,
    And chopped off his head with a shubble.


## Bones

Said Mr Smith, 'I really cannot
    Tell you, Dr Jones –
The most peculiar pain I'm in –
    I think it's in my *bones*.'

Said Dr Jones, 'Oh, Mr Smith,
    That's nothing. Without doubt
We have a simple cure for that;
    It is to take them out.'

He laid forthwith poor Mr Smith
    Close-clamped upon the table,
And, cold as stone, took out his bones
    As fast as he was able.

And Smith said, 'Thank you, thank you, *thank* you,'
    And wished him a Good-day;
And with his parcel 'neath his arm
    He slowly moved away.


## Hi!

Hi! handsome hunting man
Fire your little gun.

Bang! Now the animal
Is dead and dumb and done.
Nevermore to peep again, creep again, leap again,
Eat or sleep or drink again, Oh, what fun!


## Seeds

The seeds I sowed –
For weeks unseen –
Have pushed up pygmy
Shoots of green;
So frail you'd think
The tiniest stone
Would never let
A glimpse be shown.
But no; a pebble
Near them lies,
At least a cherry-stone
In size,
Which that mere sprout
Has heaved away,
To bask in sunshine,
See the Day.


## As I Went to the Well-Head

As I went to the well-head
I heard a bird sing:
'Lie yonder, lie yonder
The islands of Ling.

'Leagues o'er the water
Their shores are away,
In a darkness of stars,
And a foaming spray.'


## Peeping Tom

I was there – by the curtains
When some men brought a box:
And one at the house of
    Miss Emily knocks:

A low *rat-tat-tat*.
The door opened – and then,
Slowly mounting the steps, stooped
    In the strange men.

Then the door darkly shut,
And I saw their legs pass,
Like an insect's, Miss Emily's
    Window-glass –

Though why all her blinds
Have been hanging so low
These dumb foggy days,
    I don't know.

Yes, only last week
I watched her for hours,
Potting out for the winter her
    Balcony flowers.

And this very Sunday
She mused there a space,
Gazing into the street, with
    The vacantest face:

Then turned her long nose
And looked up at the skies −
One you would not have thought
    Weather-wise!

Yet . . . well, out stepped the men −
One ferrety-fair −
With gentlemen's hats, and
    Whiskers and hair;

And paused in the porch.
Then smooth, solemn, grey,
They climbed to their places,
    And all drove away

In their square varnished carriage,
The horse full of pride,
With a tail like a charger's:
    They all sate outside.

Then the road became quiet:
Her house stiff and staid −
Like a Stage − while you wait
    For the Harlequinade . . .

But what can Miss Emily
Want with a box
So long, narrow, shallow,
    And without any locks?

# The Feckless Dinner-Party

'Who are we waiting for?' '*Soup* burnt?' '. . . Eight –'
  'Only the tiniest party. – Us!'
'Darling! Divine!' 'Ten minutes late –'
  'And my digest –' 'I'm *rav*enous!'
' "Toomes"?' – 'Oh, he's new.' 'Looks crazed, I guess.'
  ' "Married" – *Again*!' 'Well; more or less!'

'Dinner is *served*!' ' "Dinner is served"!'
  'Is served?' 'Is served.' 'Ah, yes.'

'Dear Mr. Prout, will you take down
  The Lilith in leaf-green by the fire?
Blanche Ogleton? . . .' 'How coy a frown! –
  Hasn't she borrowed *Eve's* attire?'
'Morose Old Adam!' 'Charmed – I vow.'
  'Come then, and meet her now.'

'Now, Dr. Mallus – would you please? –
  Our daring poetess, Delia Seek?'
'The lady with the bony knees?'
  'And – *entre nous* – less song than beak.'
'Sharing her past with Simple Si –'
  '*Bare* facts! He'll blush!' 'Oh, fie!'

'And *you*, Sir Nathan – false but fair! –
  That fountain of wit, Aurora Pert.'
'More wit than It, poor dear! But there . . .'
  'Pitiless Pacha! *And* such a flirt!'
' "Flirt"! *Me?*' 'Who else?' 'You here . . . Who can . . .?'
  'In*corr*igible man!'

'And now, Mr. Simon – little me! –
    Last and –' 'By no means least!' 'Oh, come!
What naughty, naughty flattery!
    *Honey!* – I *hear* the creature hum!'
'Sweets for the sweet, *I* always say!'
    ' "Always"? . . . We're last.' '*This* way?' . . .

'No, sir; straight on, please.' 'I'd have vowed! –
    I came the other . . .' 'It's queer; I'm sure . . .'
'What frightful pictures!' 'Fiends!' 'The *crowd!*'
    'Such nudes!' 'I can't endure . . .'

'Yes, *there* they go.' 'Heavens! *Are* we right?'
    'Follow up closer!' ' "Prout"? – sand-blind!'
'This endless . . .' 'Who's turned down the light?'
    'Keep calm! They're close behind.'

'Oh! Dr. Mallus; what dismal stairs!'
    'I hate these old Victor . . .' 'Dry rot!'
'Darker and darker!' 'Fog!' 'The air's . . .'
    'Scarce breathable!' 'Hell!' '*What?*'

'The banister's gone!' 'It's deep; keep close!'
    'We're going down and down!' 'What fun!'
'Damp! Why, my shoes . . .' 'It's slimy . . . Not *moss!*'
    'I'm freezing cold!' 'Let's run.'

'. . . Behind us. I'm giddy. . . .' 'The catacombs . . .'
    'That shout!' 'Who's there?' 'I'm *alone*!' 'Stand back!'
'She said, Lead . . .' 'Oh!' 'Where's Toomes?' '*Toomes!*'
        'Toomes!'
    'Stifling!' 'My skull will crack!'

'Sir Nathan! *Ai!*' 'I *say! Toomes!* Prout!'
    'Where? Where?' ' "Our silks and fine array" . . .'
'She's mad.' 'I'm dying!' 'Oh, Let me *out!*'
    'My God! We've lost our way!' . . .

And now how sad-serene the abandoned house,
Whereon at dawn the spring-tide sunbeams beat;
And time's slow pace alone is ominous,
And naught but shadows of noonday therein meet;
Domestic microcosm, only a Trump could rouse:
And, pondering darkly, in the silent rooms,
He who misled them all – the butler, Toomes.


## Comfort

As I mused by the hearthside,
    Puss said to me:
'There burns the Fire, man,
    And here sit we.

'Four Walls around us
    Against the cold air;
And the latchet drawn close
    To the draughty Stair.

'A Roof o'er our heads
    Star-proof, moon immune,
And a wind in the chimney
    To wail us a tune.

'What Felicity!' miaowed he,
    'Where none may intrude;
Just Man and Beast – met
    In this Solitude!

'Dear God, what security,
  Comfort and bliss!
And to think, too, what ages
  Have brought us to this!

'You in your sheep's-wool coat,
  Buttons of bone,
And me in my fur-about
  On the warm hearthstone.'


## Good Company

The stranger from the noisy inn
Strode out into the quiet night,
Tired of the slow sea-faring men.

The wind blew fitfully in his face;
He smelt the salt, and tasted it,
In that sea-haunted, sandy place.

Dim ran the road down to the sea
Bowered in with trees, and solitary;
Ever the painted sign swang slow –
An Admiral staring moodily.

The stranger heard its silly groan;
The beer-mugs rattling to and fro;
The drawling gossip: and the glow
Streamed thro' the door on weed and stone.

Better this star-sown solitude,
The empty night-road to the sea,
Than company so dull and rude.

He smelt the nettles sour and lush,
About him went the bat's shrill cry,
Pale loomed the fragrant hawthorn-bush.

And all along the sunken road –
Green with its weeds, though sandy dry –
Bugloss, hemlock and succory –
The night-breeze wavered from the sea.
And soon upon the beach he stood.

A myriad pebbles in the faint
Horned radiance of a sinking moon
Shone like the rosary of a saint –
A myriad pebbles which, through time,
The bitter tides had visited,
Flood and ebb, by a far moon led,
Noon and night and morning-prime.

He stood and eyed the leaping sea,
The long grey billows surging on,
Baying in sullen unison
Their dirge of agelong mystery.

And, still morose, he went his way,
Over the mounded shingle strode,
And reached a shimmering sand that lay
Where transient bubbles of the froth
Like eyes upon the moonshine glowed,
Faint-coloured as the evening moth.

But not on these the stranger stared,
Nor on the stars that spanned the deep,
But on a body, flung at ease,
As if upon the shore asleep,
Hushed by the rocking seas.

Of a sudden the air was wild with cries –
Shrill and high and violent,
Fled fast a soot-black cormorant,
'Twixt ocean and the skies.

It seemed the sea was like a heart
That stormily a secret keeps
Of what it dare to none impart.
And all its waves rose, heaped and high –
And communed with the moon-grey sky.

The stranger eyed the sailor there,
Mute, and stark, and sinister –
His stiffening sea-clothes grey with salt;
His matted hair, his eyes ajar,
And glazed after the three-fold fear.

And ever the billows cried again
Over the rounded pebble stones,
Baying that heedless sailor-man.

He frowned and glanced up into the air –
Where star with star all faintly shone,
Cancer and the Scorpion,
In ancient symbol circling there:

Gazed inland over the vacant moor;
But ancient silence, and a wind
That whirls upon a sandy floor,
Were now its sole inhabitants.

Forthwith, he wheeled about – away
From the deep night's sad radiance;
The yells of gulls and cormorants
Rang shrilly in his mind.

Pursued by one who noiseless trod,
Whose sharp scythe whistled as he went,
O'er sand and shingle, tuft and sod,
Like hunted hare he coursing ran,
Nor stayed until he came again
Back to the old convivial inn –
The mugs, the smoke, the muffled din –
Packed with its slow-tongued sailor-men.


## The Railway Junction

From here through tunnelled gloom the track
Forks into two; and one of these
Wheels onward into darkening hills,
And one toward distant seas.

How still it is; the signal light
At set of sun shines palely green;
A thrush sings; other sound there's none,
Nor traveller to be seen –

Where late there was a throng. And now,
In peace awhile, I sit alone;
Though soon, at the appointed hour,
I shall myself be gone.

But not their way: the bow-legged groom,
The parson in black, the widow and son,
The sailor with his cage, the gaunt
Gamekeeper with his gun,

That fair one, too, discreetly veiled –
All, who so mutely came, and went,
Will reach those far nocturnal hills,
Or shores, ere night is spent.

I nothing know why thus we met –
Their thoughts, their longings, hopes, their fate:
And what shall I remember, except –
The evening growing late –

That here through tunnelled gloom the track
Forks into two; of these
One into darkening hills leads on,
And one toward distant seas?


## Full Circle

When thou art as little as I am, Mother,
And I as old as thou,
I'll feed thee on wild-bee honeycomb,
And milk from my cow.
I'll make thee a swan's-down bed, Mother;
Watch over thee then will I.
And if in a far-away dream you start
I'll sing thee lullaby.
It's many – Oh, ages and ages, Mother,
We've shared, we two. Soon, now:
Thou shalt be happy, grown again young,
And I as old as thou.


## Tom's Angel

No one was in the fields
But me and Polly Flint,
When, like a giant across the grass,
The flaming angel went.

It was budding time in May,
And green as green could be,
And all in his height he went along
Past Polly Flint and me.

We'd been playing in the woods,
And Polly up, and ran,
And hid her face, and said,
'Tom! Tom! The Man! The Man!'

And I up-turned; and there.
Like flames across the sky,
With wings all bristling, came
The Angel striding by.

And a chaffinch overhead
Kept whistling in the tree
While the Angel, blue as fire, came on
Past Polly Flint and me.

And I saw his hair, and all
The ruffling of his hem,
As over the clovers his bare feet
Trod without stirring them.

Polly – she cried; and, oh!
We ran, until the lane
Turned by the miller's roaring wheel,
And we were safe again.

# A Robin

Ghost-grey the fall of night,
   Ice-bound the lane,
Lone in the dying light
   Flits he again;
Lurking where shadows steal,
Perched in his coat of blood,
Man's homestead at his heel,
   Death-still the wood.

Odd restless child; it's dark;
   All wings are flown
But this one wizard's – hark!
   Stone clapped on stone!
Changeling and solitary,
Secret and sharp and small,
Flits he from tree to tree,
   Calling on all.


# The Snowdrop

Now – now, as low I stooped, thought I,
I will see what this snowdrop *is*;
So shall I put much argument by,
   And solve a lifetime's mysteries.

A northern wind had frozen the grass;
Its blades were hoar with crystal rime,
Aglint like light-dissecting glass
   At beam of morning-prime.

From hidden bulb the flower reared up
Its angled, slender, cold, dark stem,
Whence dangled an inverted cup
    For tri-leaved diadem.

Beneath these ice-pure sepals lay
A triplet of green-pencilled snow,
Which in the chill-aired gloom of day
    Stirred softly to and fro.

Mind fixed, but else made vacant, I,
Lost to my body, called my soul
To don that frail solemnity,
    Its inmost self my goal.

And though in vain – no mortal mind
Across that threshold yet hath fared! –
In this collusion I divined
    Some consciousness we shared.

Strange roads – while suns, a myriad, set –
Had led us through infinity;
And where they crossed, there then had met
    Not two of us, but three.

## Quack

What said the drake to his lady-love
    But *Quack*, then *Quack*, then QUACK!
And she, with long love-notes as sweet as his,
    Said *Quack* – then, softlier, QUACK
And Echo that lurked by the old red barn,
    Beyond their staddled stack,
Listening this love-lorn pair's delight,
    Quacked their quacked *Quack*, *Quack*, *Quacks* back.

## Oh, Yes, My Dear

Oh, yes, my dear, you have a mother,
And she, when young, was loved by another,
And in that mother's nursery
Played *her* mamma, like you and me.
When that mamma was tiny as you
She had a happy mother too:
On, on . . . Yes, presto! Puff! Pee-fee! –
And Grandam Eve and the apple-tree.
O, into distance, smalling, dimming,
Think of that endless row of women,
Like beads, like posts, like lamps, they seem –
Grey-green willows, and life a stream –
Laughing and sighing and lovely; and, oh,
You to be next in that long row!

## Seen and Heard

Lovely things these eyes have seen –
Dangling cherries in leaves dark-green;
Ducks as white as winter snow,
Which quacked as they webbed on a-row;
The wren that, with her needle note,
Through blackthorn's foam will flit and float;
Clear dews whereon the moonbeams softly gloat
    And sun will sheen.

Lovely music my ears have heard –
Catkined twigs in April stirred
By the same air that carries true
Two notes from Africa, *Cuck-oo*;
And then, when night has darkened again,
The lone wail of the willow-wren,
And cricket rasping on, 'Goode'n – goode'n',
    Shriller than mouse or bird.

Ay, and all praise would I, please God, dispose
For but one faint-hued cowslip, one wild rose.


## 'Please to Remember'

Here am I,
A poor old Guy:
Legs in a bonfire,
Head in the sky;

Shoeless my toes,
Wild stars behind,

Smoke in my nose,
And my eye-peeps blind;

Old hat, old straw –
In this disgrace;
While the wildfire gleams
On a mask for face.

Ay, all I am made of
Only trash is;
And soon – soon,
Will be dust and ashes.


## Dry August Burned

Dry August burned. A harvest hare
Limp on the kitchen table lay,
Its fur blood-blubbered, eyes astare,
While a small child that stood near by
Wept out her heart to see it there.

Sharp came the *clop* of hoofs, the clang
Of dangling chain, voices that rang.
Out like a leveret she ran,
To feast her glistening bird-clear eyes
On a team of field artillery,
Gay, to manoeuvres, thudding by.
Spur and gun and limber plate
Flashed in the sun. Alert, elate,
Noble horses, foam at lip,
Harness, stirrup, holster, whip,
She watched the sun-tanned soldiery,
Till dust-white hedge had hidden away –
Its din into a rumour thinned –

The laughing, jolting, wild array:
And then – the wonder and tumult gone –
Stood nibbling a green leaf, alone,
Her dark eyes, dreaming. . . . She turned, and ran,
Elf-like, into the house again.
The hare had vanished. . . . 'Mother,' she said,
Her tear-stained cheek now flushed with red,
'Please, may I go and see it skinned?'


## At Ease

Most wounds can Time repair;
But some are mortal – these:
For a broken heart there is no balm,
No cure for a heart at ease –

At ease, but cold as stone,
Though the intellect spin on,
And the feat and practised face may show
Nought of the life that is gone;

But smiles, as by habit taught;
And sighs, as by custom led;
And the soul within is safe from damnation,
Since it is dead.


## Clavichord

Hearken! Tiny, clear, discrete:
The listener within deems solely his,
A music so remote and sweet
It all but lovely as silence is.

# Faint Music

The meteor's arc of quiet; a voiceless rain;
The mist's mute communing with a stagnant moat;
The sigh of a flower that has neglected lain;
    That bell's unuttered note:

A hidden self rebels, its slumber broken;
Love secret as crystal forms within the womb;
The heart may as faithfully beat, the vow unspoken;
    All sounds to silence come.


# Martins: September

At secret daybreak they had met –
    Chill mist beneath the welling light
Screening the marshes green and wet –
    An ardent legion wild for flight.

Each preened and sleeked an arrowlike wing;
    Their eager throats with lapsing cries
Praising whatever fate might bring –
    Cold wave, or Africa's paradise.

Unventured, trackless leagues of air;
    England's sweet summer narrowing on;
Her lovely pastures: nought their care –
    Only this ardour to be gone.

A tiny, elfin, ecstatic host . . .
    And 'neath them, on the highway's crust,
Like some small mute belated ghost,
    A sparrow pecking in the dust.

# Swallows Flown

Whence comes that small continuous silence
   Haunting the livelong day?
This void, where a sweetness, so seldom heeded,
   Once ravished my heart away?
As if a loved one, too little valued,
   Had vanished – could not stay?


# The Old Summerhouse

This blue-washed, old, thatched summerhouse –
Paint scaling, and fading from its walls –
How often from its hingeless door
I have watched – dead leaf, like the ghost of a mouse,
Rasping the worn brick floor –
The snows of the weir descending below,
And their thunderous waterfall.

Fall – fall: dark, garrulous rumour,
Until I could listen no more.
Could listen no more – for beauty with sorrow
Is a burden hard to be borne:
The evening light on the foam, and the swans, there;
That music, remote, forlorn.

## Rooks in October

They sweep up, crying, riding the wind,
   Ashen on blue outspread –
Gilt-lustred wing, sharp light-glazed beak,
   And low flat ravenous head.

Claws dangling, down they softly swoop
   Out of the eastern sun
Into the yellowing green-leaved boughs –
   Their morning feast begun.

Clasping a twig that even a linnet
   Might bend in song, they clip
Pat from the stalked embossed green cup
   Its fruitage bitter-ripe.

Oh, what divine far hours their beauty
   Of old for me beguiled,
When – acorn, oak, untarnished heavens –
   I watched them as a child!


## The Last Arrow

There came a boy,
Full quiver on his back –
Tapped at my door ajar.

'No, no, my child,' said I,
'I nothing lack;
And see! – the evening star!'

Finger on string,
His dangerous eyes
Gazed boldly into mine:

'Know thou my mother
An Immortal is!
Guard thee, and hope resign!'

'But patience,' I pleaded,
Pointing to a shelf,
Where rusting arrows lay.

'All these, times gone,
You squandered on myself,
Why come – so late, to-day?'

These words scarce uttered,
I discerned a Shade
Shadow till then had hid;

*Clang* went that bowstring,
And past wit to evade,
Into my bosom slid

His final dart.
He shook his rascal head,
Its curls by the lamp-shine gilt:

'Thank thou the Gods!
Here's One, I vow,' he said,
'Not even thee shall jilt.'

# Snow

This meal-white snow –
Oh, look at the bright fields!
What crystal manna
Death-cold winter yields!

Falling from heavens
Earth knows little of,
Yet mantling it
As with a flawless love –

A shining cloak –
It to the naked gives,
Wooing all sorrow
From the soul it shrives.

Adam no calmer vales
Than these descried;
Leda a shadow were
This white beside.

Water stays still for wonder;
Herb and flower,
Else starved with cold,
In warmth and darkness cower.

Miracle, far and near,
That starry flake
Can of its myriads
Such wide pastures make,

For sun to colour,
And for moon to wan,
And day's vast vault of blue
To arch upon!

A marvel of light,
Whose verge of radiance seems
Frontier of paradise,
The bourne of dreams.

O tranquil, silent, cold –
Such loveliness to see:
The heart sighs answer,
*Benedicite!*


## Crops

Farmer Giles has cut his rye;
    Oh my! Oh my!
Farmer Bates has cut his wheat;
    Och, the thieving hares in it!

Farmer Turvey's cut his barley;
    Ripe and early, ripe and early.
And where day breaks, rousing not,
    Farmer Weary's cut his throat.


## Done For

Old Ben Bailey
He's been and done

For a small brown bunny
With his long gun.

Glazed are the eyes
That stared so clear,
And no sound stirs
In that hairy ear.

What was once beautiful
Now breathes not,
Bound for Ben Bailey's
Smoking pot.


## The Old Sailor

There came an old sailor
Who sat to sup
Under the trees
Of the *Golden Cup*.

Beer in a mug
And a slice of cheese
With a hunk of bread
He munched at his ease.

Then in the summer
Dusk he lit
A little black pipe,
And sucked at it.

He thought of his victuals,
Of ships, the sea,
Of his home in the West,
And his children three.

And he stared and stared
To where, afar,
The lighthouse gleamed
At the harbour bar;

Till his pipe grew cold,
And down on the board
He laid his head,
And snored, snored, snored.


## Pooh!

Dainty Miss Apathy
Sat on a sofa,
Dangling her legs,
And with nothing to do;
She looked at a drawing of
Old Queen Victoria,
At a rug from far Persia –
An exquisite blue;
At a bowl of bright tulips;
A needlework picture
Of doves caged in wicker
You could almost hear coo;
She looked at the switch
That evokes e-
Lectricity;
At the coals of an age
B.C. millions and two –
When the trees were like ferns
And the reptiles all flew;
She looked at the cat

Asleep on the hearthrug,
At the sky at the window, –
The clouds in it, too;
And a marvellous light
From the West burning through:
And the one silly word
In her desolate noddle
As she dangled her legs,
Having nothing to do,
Was not, as you'd guess,
Of dumbfoundered felicity,
But contained just four letters,
And these pronounced *POOH!*


## Ever

Ever, ever
Stir and shiver
The reeds and rushes
By the river:
Ever, ever,
As if in dream,
The lone moon's silver
Sleeks the stream.
What old sorrow,
What lost love,
Moon, reeds, rushes,
Dream you of?

## Lob-Lie-by-the-Fire

Keep me a crust
Or starve I must;
Hoard me a bone
Or I am gone;
A handful of coals
Leave red for me;
Or the smouldering log
Of a wild-wood tree;
Even a kettle
To sing on the hob
Will comfort the heart
Of poor old Lob:
Then with his hairy
Hands he'll bless
Prosperous master,
And kind mistress.


## The Snowflake

Before I melt,
Come, look at me!
This lovely icy filigree!
Of a great forest
In one night
I make a wilderness
Of white:
By skyey cold
Of crystals made,
All softly, on

Your finger laid,
I pause, that you
My beauty see:
Breathe, and I vanish
Instantly.


## The Bead Mat

We had climbed the last steep flight of stairs;
    Alone were she and I:
'It's something I wanted to give to you,'
    She whispered, with a sigh.

There, in her own small room she stood –
    Where the last beam of sun
Burned in the glass – and showed me what
    For me she had done: –

An oblong shining mat of beads,
    Yellow and white and green,
And where the dark-blue middle was
    A gold between.

I heard no far-off voice, no sound:
    Only her clear grey eyes
Drank in the thoughts that in my face
    Passed shadow-wise.

She clasped her hands, and turned her head,
    And in the watchful glass
She saw how many things had seen
    All that had passed.

She snatched her gift away; her cheek
    With scarlet was aflame;
'It isn't *any*thing,' she said,
        If *we*'re the same!'

Her eyes were like a stormy sea,
    Forlorn, and vast, and grey;
Wherein a little beaten ship
        Flew through the spray.


## The Border Bird

As if a voice had called, I woke,
The world in silence lay;
The winter sun was not yet up,
The moon still in the sky.

A strange sea bird had hither flown,
Out of the last of night,
While yet the Dog Star in the west
Shone palely bright.

His wings came like a *hush* of wind,
His feet were coral red,
No mantling swan has softer down,
No blackcap blacker head.

He lighted on the frozen snow;
Trod here, and there, and then
Lifted his gentle neck and gazed
Up at my window-pane.

And I, from out of dream, looked down,
This lovely thing to see;
The world a wilderness of white,
Nought living there but he.

Then with a sweet low call, he raised
Dark head and pinions wan,
Swept up into the gold of day,
    Was gone.


## The Song of Seven

Far away, and long ago –
May sweet Memory be forgiven!
Came a Wizard in the evening,
And he sang the Song of Seven.
Yes, he plucked his jangling harp-strings
With fingers smooth and even;
And his eyes beneath his dangling hair
Were still as is the sea;
But the Song of Seven has never yet,
One note, come back to me.

The Song of One I know,
A rose its thorns between;

The Song of Two I learned
Where only the birds have been;

The Song of Three I heard
When March was fleet with hares;

The Song of Four was the wind's – the wind's,
Where wheat grew thick with tares;

The Song of Five, ah me!
Lovely the midmost one;

The Song of Six, died out
Before the dream was done. . . .

One – two – three – four – five, six –
And all the grace notes given:
But *widdershins*, and witchery-sweet,
Where is the Song of Seven?


## Will-o'-the-Wisp

'Will-o'-the-Wisp,
Come out of the fen,
And vex no more
Benighted men!'
Pale, blue,
Wavering, wan,
'Will-o'-the-Wisp,
Begone, begone!'

But the trees weep,
The mist-drops hang,
Light dwindles
The bents among.
Oh, and he hovers,
Oh, and he flies,
Will-o'-the-Wisp,
With the baleful eyes.

# Nothing

*Whsst*, and away, and over the green,
Scampered a shape that never was seen.
It ran without sound, it ran without shadow,
Never a grass-blade in unmown meadow
Stooped at the thistledown fall of its foot.
I watched it vanish, yet saw it not –
A moment past, it had gazed at me;
Now nought but myself and the spindle tree.
A nothing! – Of air? Of earth? Of sun? –
From emptiness come, into vacancy gone! . . .
*Whsst*, and away, and over the green,
Scampered a shape that never was seen.


# Then as Now

Then as Now; and Now as Then,
Spins on this World of Men.
White – Black – Yellow – Red:
They wake, work, eat, play, go to bed.
Black – Yellow – Red – White:
They talk, laugh, weep, dance, morn to night.
Yellow – Red – White – Black:
Sun shines, moon rides, clouds come back.
Red – White – Black – Yellow:
Count your hardest, who could tell o'
The myriads that have come and gone,
Stayed their stay this earth upon,
And vanished then, their labour done?

Sands of the wilderness, stars in heaven,
Solomon could not sum them even:
Then as Now; Now as Then
Still spins on this World of Men.


## Under the Rose
### *The Song of the Wanderer*

Nobody, nobody told me
What nobody, nobody knows:
But now I know where the Rainbow ends,
*I* know where there grows
A Tree that's called the Tree of Life,
I know where there flows
The River of All-Forgottenness,
And where the Lotus blows,
And I – I've trodden the forest, where
In flames of gold and rose,
To burn, and then arise again,
    The Phoenix goes.

Nobody, nobody told me
What nobody, nobody knows:
Hide thy face in a veil of light,
Put on thy silver shoes,
Thou art the Stranger I know best,
Thou art the sweet heart, who
Came from the Land between Wake and Dream,
Cold with the morning dew.

## Israfel

*To Alec McLaren*
*1940*

Sleepless I lay, as the grey of dawn
Through the cold void street stole into the air,
When, in the hush, a solemn voice
Pealed suddenly out in Connaught Square.

Had I not heard notes wild as these
A thousand times in childhood ere
This chill March daybreak they awoke
The echoing walls of Connaught Square,

I might have imagined a seraph – strange
In such bleak days! – had deigned to share,
For joy and love, the haunts of man –
An Israfel in Connaught Square!

Not that this singer eased the less
A human heart surcharged with care –
Merely a blackbird, London-bred,
Warbling of Spring in Connaught Square!

It was the contrast with a world
Of darkness, horror, grief, despair,
Had edged with an irony so sharp
That rapturous song in Connaught Square.


## The Burning-Glass

No map shows my Jerusalem,
   No history my Christ;

Another language tells of them,
    A hidden evangelist.

Words may create rare images
    Within their narrow bound;
'Twas speechless childhood brought me these,
    As music may, in sound.

Yet not the loveliest song that ever
    Died on the evening air
Could from my inmost heart dissever
    What life had hidden there.

It is the blest reminder of
    What earth in shuddering bliss
Nailed on a cross – that deathless Love –
    Through all the eternities.

I am the Judas whose perfidy
    Sold what no eye hath seen,
The rabble in dark Gethsemane,
    And Mary Magdalene.

To very God who day and night
    Tells me my sands out-run,
I cry in misery infinite,
    'I am thy long-lost son.'


# Swifts
  *1943*


No; they are only birds – swifts, in the loft of the morning,
Coursing, disporting, courting, in the pale-blue arc of the sky.
There is no venom for kin or for kind in their wild-winged
    archery,

Nor death in their innocent droppings as fleet in their
   mansions they fly;
Swooping, with flicker of pinion to couple, the loved with
   the loved one,
Never with malice or hate, in their vehement sallies through
   space.
Listen! that silken rustle, as they charge on their beehive
   houses,
Fashioned of dried-up mud daubed each in its chosen place.
Hunger – not fear – sharps the squawk of their featherless
   nestlings;
From daybreak into the dark their circuitings will not cease:
How beautiful they! – and the feet on earth's heavenly
   mountains
Of him that bringeth good tidings, proclaimeth the gospel of
   peace!


## The Field

Yes, there was once a battle here:
There, where the grass takes on a shade
Of paradisal green, sun-clear –
   There the last stand was made.


## The Blind Boy

A spider her silken gossamer
In the sweet sun began to wind;
The boy, alone in the window-seat,
   Saw nought of it. He was blind.

By a lustre of glass a slender ray
Was shattered into a myriad tints –
Violet, emerald, primrose, red –
   Light's exquisite finger-prints.

Unmoved, his face in the shadow stayed,
Rapt in a reverie mute and still.
The ray stole on; but into that mind
   No gem-like atom fell.

It paused to ponder upon a moth,
Snow-hooded, delicate past belief,
Drowsing, a spelican from his palm . . .
   O child of tragedy – if

Only a moment you might gaze out
On this all-marvellous earth we share! . . .
A smile stole into the empty eye,
   And features fair,

As if an exquisite whisper of sound.
Of source as far in time and space,
And, no less sovran than light, had found
   Its recompense in his face.


## The Owl

Owl of the wildwood I:
Muffled in sleep I drowse,
Where no fierce sun in heaven
Can me arouse.

My haunt's a hollow
In a half-dead tree.

Whose strangling ivy
Shields and shelters me.

But when dark's starlight
Thrids my green domain,
My plumage trembles and stirs,
I wake again:

A spectral moon
Silvers the world I see;
Out of their daylong lairs
Creep thievishly

Night's living things.
Then I,
Wafted away on soundless pinions
Fly;
Curdling her arches
With my hunting-cry:

*A-hooh! a-hooh:*
Four notes; and then,
Solemn, sepulchral, cold,
Four notes again,
The listening dingles
Of my woodland through:
*A-hooh! A-hooh! –*
    *A-hooh!*


## Once

Once would the early sun steal in through my eastern
    window,
            A sea of time ago;

Tracing a stealthy trellis of shadow across the pictures
        With his gilding trembling glow;
Brimming my mind with rapture, as though of some alien
  spirit,
        In those eternal hours
I spent with my self as a child; alone, in a world of wonder –
        Air, and light and flowers;
Tenderness, longing, grief, intermingling with bodiless beings
        Shared else with none:
How would desire flame up in my soul; with what
  passionate yearning
        As the rays stole soundlessly on! –
Rays such as Rembrandt adored, such as dwell on the faces
  of seraphs,
        Wings-folded, solemn head,
Piercing the mortal with sorrow past all comprehension. . . .

        Little of that I read
In those shadowy runes in my bedroom. But one wild notion
        Made my heart with tears overflow –
The knowledge that love unsought, unspoken, unshared,
  unbetokened,
        Had mastered me through and through:
And yet – the children we are! – that naught of its ardour
  and beauty
        Even the loved should know.


## The Dead Jay

    A witless, pert, bedizened fop,
        Man scoffs, resembles you:
    Fate levels all – voice harsh or sweet –
        Ringing the woodlands through:

But, O, poor hapless bird, that broken death-stilled wing,
    That miracle of blue!


## Eureka

Lost in a dream last night was I.
I dreamed that, from this earth set free,
In some remote futurity
I had reached the place prepared for me.

A vault, it seemed, of burnished slate,
Whose planes beyond the pitch of sight
Converged – unswerving, immaculate –
Bathed in a haze of blinding light;

Not of the sun, or righteousness.
No cherub here, o'er lute-string bowed,
Tinkled some silly hymn of peace,
But, 'Silence! No loitering allowed!'

In jet-black characters I read
Incised upon the porcelain floor.
Ay, and the silence of the dead
No sentient heart could harrow more.

There, stretching far as eye could see,
Beneath that flat and leprous glare
A maze of immense machinery
Hummed in the ozoned air –

Prodigious wheels of steel and brass;
And – ranged along the un-windowed walls –
Engrossed in objects of metal and glass,
Stooped spectres, in spotless over-alls.

Knees quaking, dazed affrighted eyes,
I turned to the Janitor and cried,
'Is this, friend, Hell or Paradise?'
And, sneering, he replied,

'Terms trite as yours the ignorant
On earth, it seems, may yet delude.
Here, "sin" and "saint" and "hierophant"
Share exile with "the Good".

'Be grateful that the state of bliss
Henceforth, perhaps, reserved for thee,
Is sane and sanative as this,
And void of fatuous fantasy.

'Here God, the Mechanist, reveals,
As only mechanism can,
Mansions to match the new ideals
Of his co-worker, Man.

'On strict probation, you are now
To toil with yonder bloodless moles –
These skiagrams will show you how –
On mechanizing human souls . . .'

At this I woke: and, cold as stone,
Lay quaking in the hazardous light
    Of earth's familiar moon;
A clothes-moth winged from left to right,
    A tap dripped on and on;
And there, my handmade pot, my jug
Beside the old grained washstand stood;
There, too, my once-gay threadbare rug,
    The flattering moonlight wooed:
And – Heaven forgive a dream-crazed loon! –
    I found them very good.

# Birds in Winter

I know not what small winter birds these are,
Warbling their hearts out in that dusky glade
While the pale lustre of the morning star
   In heaven begins to fade.

Not me they sing for, this – earth's shortest – day,
A human listening at his window-glass;
They would, affrighted, cease and flit away
   At glimpse even of my face.

And yet how strangely mine their music seems,
As if of all things loved my heart was heir,
Had helped create them – albeit in my dreams –
   And they disdained my share.


# Empty

The house by the sand dunes
Was bleached and dark and bare;
Birds, in the sea-shine,
Silvered and shadowed the air.

I called at the shut door,
I tirled at the pin:
Weeks – weeks of woesome tides,
The sand had drifted in.

The sand had heaped itself about
In the wefting of the wind;
And knocking never summoned ghost;
And dreams none can find

Like coins left at full of flood,
Gold jetsam of the sea.
Salt that water, bitter as love,
That will let nothing be

Unfevered, calm and still,
Like an ageing moon in the sky
Lighting the eyes of daybreak –
With a wick soon to die.

What then was shared there,
Who's now to tell?
Horizon-low the sea-borne light,
And dumb the buoyed bell.


## 'Said Flores'

'If I had a drop of attar
And a clot of wizard clay,
Birds we would be with wings of light
And fly to Cathay.

'If I had the reed called Ozmadoom,
And skill to cut pen,
I'd float a music into the air –
You'd listen, and then . . .

'If that small moon were mine for lamp,
I would look, I would see
The silent thoughts, like silver fish,
You are thinking of me.

'There is nothing upon grass or ground,
In the mountains or the skies,

But my heart faints in longing for,
And the tears drop from my eyes.

'And if I ceased from pining –
What buds were left to blow?
Where the wild swan? Where the wood-dove?
Where *then* should I go?'


## Joy

This little wayward boy
Stretched out his hands to me,
Saying his name was Joy;
Saying all things that seem
Tender, and wise, and true
Never need fade while he
Drenches them through and through
With his sweet mastery;
Told me that Love's clear eyes
Pools were without the sky,
Earth, without paradise,
Were he not nigh;
Even that grief conceals
Him in a dark disguise;
And that affliction brings
    All it denies.

Not mine to heed him then –
Till fell the need – and Oh,
All his sweet converse gone,
Where could I go?
What could I do? –
But seek him up and down,

Thicket and thorn and fell,
Till night in gloom came on
Unpierceable?
Then, when all else must fail,
Stepped from the dark to me,
Voiced like the nightingale,
Masked, weeping, he.


## Solitude

When the high road
   Forks into a by-road,
And that drifts into a lane,
And the lane breaks into a bridle-path,
   A chace forgotten
   Still as death,
And green with the long night's rain;
Through a forest winding on and on,
Moss, and fern, and sun-bleached bone,
   Till only a trace remain;
And that dies out in a waste of stone
A bluff of cliff, vast, trackless, wild,
Blue with the harebell, undefiled;
Where silence enthralls the empty air,
Mute with a presence unearthly fair,
      And a path is sought
         In vain. . . .

It is then the Ocean
   Looms into sight,
A gulf enringed with a burning white,
A sea of sapphire, dazzling bright;

And islands,
    Peaks of such beauty that
Bright danger seems to lie in wait,
Dread, disaster, boding fate;
And soul and sense are appalled thereat;
Though an Ariel music on the breeze
Thrills the mind with a lorn unease,
Cold with all mortal mysteries.
        And every thorn,
        And weed, and flower,
    And every time-worn stone
A challenge cries on the trespasser:
        *Beware!*
        *Thou art alone!*


## Martins

    '*Chelidon urbica urbica!*'
    I cried on the little bird,
Meticulously enunciating each syllable of each word;
    '*Chelidon urbica urbica!*'
    Listen to me, I plead!
  There are swallows all snug in the hayloft,
  I have all that your nestlings can need –
  Shadow and sunshine and sweet shallow water –
  Come, build in my eaves, and breed!

  Fly high, my love! My love, fly low!
  I watched the sweet pretty creatures go –
  Floating, skimming, and wheeling so
  Swiftly and softly – like flakes of snow,
'Gainst the dark of the cedar-boughs, to and fro: . . .

But no!
But no!
'*Chelidon urbica urbica!*'
None paid me the faintest heed.


## The Plaster Cast

It called to mind one now long out of sight,
Whom love still treasures with its secret grace:
That cast – half-hidden there – sepulchral white,
A random moonbeam on its peaceful face.


## The Last Swallow

The robin whistles again. Day's arches narrow.
Tender and quiet skies lighten the withering flowers.
The dark of winter must come. . . . But that tiny arrow,
Circuiting high in the blue – the year's last swallow,
Knows where the coast of far mysterious sun-wild Africa lours.


## The Spotted Flycatcher

Gray on gray post, this silent little bird
Swoops on its prey – prey neither seen nor heard!
A click of bill; a flicker; and, back again!
Sighs Nature an *Alas*? Or merely, *Amen*?

# Blondin

With clinging dainty catlike tread,
His pole in balance, hand to hand,
And, softly smiling, into space
He ventures on that threadlike strand.

Above him is the enormous sky,
Beneath, a frenzied torrent roars,
Surging where massed Niagara
Its snow-foamed arc of water pours:

But he, with eye serene as his
Who sits in daydream by the fire,
His every sinew, bone and nerve
Obedient to his least desire,

Treads softly on, with light-drawn breath,
Each inch-long toe, precisely pat,
In inward trust, past wit to probe –
This death-defying acrobat! . . .

Like some old Saint on his old rope-bridge,
Between another world and this,
Dead-calm 'mid inward vortices,
Where little else but danger is.


# Slim Cunning Hands

Slim cunning hands at rest, and cozening eyes –
Under this stone one loved too wildly lies;
How false she was, no granite could declare;
    Nor all earth's flowers, how fair.

## 'It Was The Last Time He Was Seen Alive'

'You saw him, then? . . . That very night?'
'A moment only. As I passed by.

'The lane goes down into shadow there,
And the sycamore boughs meet overhead;
Then bramble and bracken everywhere,
Moorland, whin, and the wild instead.
But the jasmined house is painted white
    And so reflects the sky.

'He was standing alone in the dwindling dusk,
Close to the window – that rapt, still face,
And hair a faded grey –
Apparently lost in thought; as when
The past seeps into one's mind again,
With its memoried hopes and joys, and pain,
And seduces one back . . .

            'He stirred, and then
Caught sight, it seemed, of the moon in the west –
Like a waif in the heavens astray –
Smiled, as if at her company;
Folded his old hands over his breast;
Bowed: and then went his way.'


## Winter Evening

Over the wintry fields the snow drifts; falling, falling;
    Its frozen burden filling each hollow. And hark;
    Out of the naked woods a wild bird calling,
        On the starless verge of the dark!

## An Old Cannon

Come, patient rust;
Come, spider with thy loom,
Make of this enginery,
War's dateless tomb!

Frail bindweed, clamber, and cling,
And clog this motionless wheel;
Upon its once hot throat
Hoar-frost, congeal!

O, may its thunder have won
A last surcease,
And its dark mouth of woe
Ever yet hollower grow
In praise of peace!


## In a Churchyard

As children, told to go to bed,
Puff out their candle's light,
Knowing earth's natural dark is best
Wherein to take their flight
Into the realms of sleep: – so we
God's summons did obey;
Not without fear our tired eyes shut,
And now await the day.

## Tarbury Steep

The moon in her gold over Tarbury Steep
    Wheeled full, in the hush of the night,
To rabbit and hare she gave her chill beams
    And to me on that silvery height.

From the dusk of its glens thrilled the nightjar's strange cry,
    A peewit wailed over the wheat,
Else still was the air, though the stars in the sky
    Seemed with music in beauty to beat.

O many a mortal has sat there before,
    Since its chalk lay in shells in the sea,
And the ghosts that looked out of the eyes of them all
    Shared Tarbury's moonlight with me.

And many, as transient, when I have gone down,
    To the shades and the silence of sleep,
Will gaze, lost in dream, on the loveliness seen
    In the moonshine of Tarbury Steep.


## Ulladare

Down by thy waters, Ulladare,
    A cedar gloomy and profound
Bids the north wind awaken there
    How sad a sound!

No exile's harp-strings could entice
    Sorrow so heedfully as this
To wake with music memories
    Of bygone bliss.

Then what far peace, to me unknown,
   Seems, by that gently lipping wave,
That shrouded tree to brood upon,
   Unless the grave?

## De Profundis

The metallic weight of iron;
The glaze of glass;
The inflammability of wood . . .

You will not be cold there;
You will not wish to see your face in a mirror;
There will be no heaviness,
Since you will not be able to lift a finger.

There will be company, but they will not heed you;
Yours will be a journey only of two paces
Into view of the stars again; but you will not make it.

There will be no recognition;
No one, who should see you, will say –
Throughout the uncountable hours –

'Why . . . the last time we met, I brought you some flowers!'

## The Minstrel

'Black night; small moon;
Stars needle-clear.
I sing a song:
To bring you cheer.'

'Away, away!
These walls are dumb –
Minstrel, not here
Song-singing come.'

'That voice sighs soft
As whispering bough?
Sing I more clearly –
Hearken, now!'

'Minstrel begone!
'Tis not night's breath
Sighs in thine ear:
I am death.'


## Tat for Tit

Shrill, glass-clear notes – 'Titmouse!' I sighed, enchanted;
Then looked for the singer ere its song should cease:
A wild-eyed gipsy pushing an old go-cart,
    Its wheels in need of grease.


## The China Cat

You never stir, and heaven forbid,
Since, mutest companion, if you did –
A creature formed of clay and glaze –
Nature herself would stand at gaze,
Albeit it with an intent to flatter:
Man would have conjured life from matter –
If from your bowels there should befall
A low protracted caterwaul,

Those slanting eyes should open and pause,
Those pads eject their hidden claws.
No nightlong vigil I know well
Would consummate that miracle;
Yet even that passive attitude
Once did a questing dog delude.


## Le Jeu est Fait

Here lies a gambler, every trick now played –
Diamonds useless; his last Heart mislaid;
By some blind lank-faced Knave of Clubs betrayed;
    And only one card left, a Spade.